PHENOMENAL WOMAN HELP WITH CO-DEPENDENCY, TOXIC RELATIONSHIPS, AND TRANSFORMATION

By Anntoinette Louis Joy

Table of Contents

Dedication

To God first, my family and friends who encouraged me to follow my heart and dream fiercely!

Acknowledgments

I am a phenomenal woman, and I had you notice I said I had, as in the past tense, severe co-dependency issues all my adult life. I was in and out of destructive relationships as well. It stemmed from childhood trauma, and I will go into that further in this book. Finally, with assistance from family, God, and friends, I had therapy with a trained domestic violence counselor, which turned my life around. I am now living my best life ever, Praise the Lord. I was broken, but no longer have I been healed. Praise God! If you're in a destructive relationship and don't know how to go forth, I pray this book will help you!

For those of you who are not familiar with me, I am a co-dependent healing woman, and I am recovering from a life of co-dependency. Some of you may not know co-dependency, and I will attempt to clarify this meaning in this book. Get some help, please, if you begin to understand that toxic, dysfunctional, narcissistic men are destructive, and he will destroy you, for he will make your life a living HELL, trust me because that was what happened to me. I would still be in that dysfunctional relationship if I had not got some counseling. So, this book is dedicated to women like me who may be suffering from co-dependency or unhappy relationships and can't figure out how it happened. But, with prayer, counseling, and support from family and friends, you can overcome this co-dependency. Just ask God not to move your mountain. Just give you the strength to climb that mountain instead!

About the Author

Lives in Georgia, s married, and has three daughters and grandkids. Her hobbies include music, reading and writing, and attending church.

Chapter 1
What is Co-dependency and How Did I Get It?

That is a good question; if you already know the answer, that is fantastic, but the truth is most of us do not know what it is, but we're living as co-dependent women. We're living with a man who disrespects us, treats us like a dog, and will not work or marry. Something is wrong with that picture, and you? I'm sorry we may be phenomenal women, but even strong women must go through things to become strong. This is one of those trials and tribulations that make you strong in James 1:2-type situations. But this trial will only benefit you if you have been healed from past pains, especially childhood ones.

It took me a while to heal with therapy; it is a continuous process and is ongoing. Therapy offers a non-judgmental, caring, and compassionate environment, thus facilitating your healing process. It also helps you regain your lost identity, confused and tangled up as a child. Therapy enables you to grow your self-esteem and self-worth. You saw I said grow it because the growth of your self-esteem and self-worth were stunted due to childhood traumas (rape, abuse, abandonment, etc.). You gain ownership of your feelings, desires, wants, and needs and can now verbalize them. You can tell a man what you will and won't do. Previously, before therapy, you couldn't do that primarily due to your co-dependency. You will gain the strength to walk away from harmful, toxic, unfulfilling, and abusive relationships. You can gift a toxic narcissistic man with a bye, next (my favorite), or keep it moving!

You turn your anger and frustrations on yourself without some help or therapy. As co-dependent women, we don't know how to emotionally disconnect and even avoid romantic relationships with narcissistic men. You see, these men match our passive, submissive, self-sacrificing self. We find narcissistic men charming, bold, confident, and domineering. We give up our power, letting the narcissistic man control and manipulate us. And we think he could really love and care about us.

Wrong again, it's the co-dependency masquerading as love!

The definition of co-dependency, according to Wikipedia.org, is that it's a concept that you have an excessive emotional or Psychological reliance on someone, typically someone who needs your support because of an illness, addiction, alcoholism, poor mental health, immaturity, irresponsible or underachievement that undermines your relationship.

In other words, they use you for selfish reasons, like a nice new car to drive around without paying for it. Or a warm, cozy home like you live in again, not having to pay for it or help you pay for it; after all, it's your house, not *his*. You supply him with your money for their addictions to alcohol, drugs, and women, all freely given to them by *YOU*. The only thing he must do is sleep with you with no other requirements to be with you! Does that sound about right? He brings nothing to the table except a big tool! You get the picture. They are pickup men: they do it for a living. A tool man works with a tool, like a carpenter; his job depends on the tools he uses. Same thing in a different scenario, but you get the point! They ride around looking for victims to pick up, and that's a relatively easy task if you know the right things to say to a lonely, low self-esteem, sometimes unattractive, usually overweight woman like I was; that could also be You! If that's all a man must do to be with you, there is something wrong with that picture. It's wrong, and yes, you suffer from co-dependency.

There are three stages to co-dependency: early, middle, and late. Stage one is called the early stage, in which co-dependent women become more and more obsessed with a toxic, dysfunctional man. We get lost in our desire to please him to do anything for him. We cook, clean up, buy him things, and give him our hard-earned money.

And for what reason? Oh, yeah, we're broken! We give up our kids, parents, family, and friends for this man. That's how someone can tell you to be co-dependent.

Stage two, or the middle stage, starts when you become more and more anxious and guilty and blame yourself for giving up everything, as well as doing everything for this toxic man.

You already suffer from low self-esteem, which plummets because you realize he isn't doing anything for YOU! No thank you, no appreciation, nothing! That's what my ex-husband did. NOTHING! At this point, you're getting frustrated, angry, and resentful while trying to change this fool! You begin to nag him or blame him and even try manipulating any and everything to get this fool to make you feel good about the sacrifices you've made for him. So, to cover up his ignorant behavior, we lie to family, friends, and even co-workers. While he's at your house chilling, he doesn't work anywhere; we make up excuses like he is looking for a job or was laid off due to COVID! Then we start to self-medicate using alcohol, drugs (commonly weed or cocaine), not eating correctly, missing meals, gambling, increased shopping, and running up bills. Your behavior increases as well of dependency, clinging to him, compliant whatever he wants or needs, and so on. You're a mess and need much help at this point.

The last stage of co-dependency is called the late stage. As it implies, it affects your mental health as well as physical health too. You start having stress-related symptoms like insomnia, high blood pressure, headaches, muscle pains, digestive problems, eating disorders, and heart disease. If you're self-medicating with alcohol or drugs, it gets worse as well. The little bit of your self-esteem or self-worth goes out the window, causing severe depression. You feel helpless, hopeless, depressed, angry, trapped, and have hit ROCK BOTTOM! You need an intervention called therapy! If this sounds like something you're going through, please get help! I suffered from co-dependency and had therapy, which turned my life around, and you can too!

You let your looks go down the drain, speak, and look torn up from the floor up, and you know this: that's why you let this guy take advantage of your passiveness. Yet you continue to say, "I can't find a good man"! When I married a good man four years ago, many co-workers asked me, "How'd you do it? Do what, I answered. Then they replied, "Get such a good man!" After I told them about my dieting, exercise with a trainer, diet modifications, and skin care with Mary Kay, they just stared at me. Then they made remarks like, "I can't do all that," or "Oh!" So, in other words, the stuff I did for me was too much. What the HELL! I loved myself and nourished myself, took care of my health and appearance, and because of that, attracted some not toxic nor dysfunctional good men. This particular one was my soul mate. If I can do it, how come you can't? All that usually stems from co-dependency issues and past traumas, which manifest in you as lonely, overweight, with low self-esteem and no self-worth. I know because that was me before therapy!

Several co-workers had toolmen at home; I'm sure you know some, too. They didn't work anywhere and weren't worried about working because these co-workers were women who were overweight, desperate, lonely, and co-dependent. And these guys took them through hoops, and one of my co-workers men had the nerve to cheat on her, too! She told me once, "All men cheat!" I looked her up and down and commented, "All YOUR men cheat on you because you ALLOW them too!" Now, she was a young woman in her forties! This was the only type of men she knew of were tool men. Get in, take all your shit, use you get out, and move on to the next victim.

And there is no age limit, color, or nationality again. You're not alone. It happens to all of us broken women with low self-esteem and no self-worth! He had the nerve to even cheat on her multiple times and gave her an STD (sexually transmitted disease). She still stayed with his cheating ass!' I would have been kicking his no-working ass out of my house! Because that is what I did divorce the jackass I was married to when I found out he was cheating on me. I may have been co-dependent and lonely, but I was not a fool or stupid! Don't underestimate a good woman and think you can pull the wool over her eyes because she's lonely! Nope! Not me, but obviously, like my co-worker, some desperate women take it because in their mind (devil convinced) them to think they can't do any better than a tool man!

They look in the mirror and are not pleased with the person who looks back at them. Hair is unkempt, in a ponytail or gray, facial wrinkles or dull skin, yellowed teeth, fat, yes, I said. Call me an ass, it is true, for that was my description before I got tired of looking like that and decided that only I could make that step to transform my life. Stop denying the truth, for you can lie to others, but at least be honest with yourself! And I felt the same way: why couldn't I get a good man NEITHER! Well, you've got to do more than wish; although wishes come true, mine did. But you've also got to do your part to become a REALITY! And I did my homework. It's called transformation 'HALLELUJAH!' To get a good man, you've got to attract him with your APPEARANCE! Men are visual; they look at you, and if they like what they see and believe you, they will try to get your attention and phone number. Now the ball is in your court; you can accept the attention or decline like I did if they did not appeal to me!

Co-dependent women give more of themselves than their partners give back to them. What they hope for is that this narcissistic man will eventually understand their needs, which they never do! You see, we co-dependent women get mixed up and confused when we think of caretaking and sacrificing with loyalty and love. Again, it is not love; it is co-dependency! We're proud of our unwavering love and dedication to the narcissistic man.

On the other hand, they couldn't care less. They couldn't give a damn! We co-independent women long for and need love, but because he's a jackass, my big narcissistic guy, this is a dream because that is all it is, a goal that will never happen. Because this dream never occurred to me, I became silently bitter, angry, frustrated, and more unhappy than I was.

We get stuck in a pattern of sacrificing and giving without the possibility of ever receiving the same back from these narcissistic men. Your low self-esteem, low self-worth, and pessimism manifest in the form of learned helplessness that keeps you in these toxic, dysfunctional relationships.

On the other hand, the narcissistic man loves this relationship. He gets to be powerful, competent, and appreciated by YOU! He loves the fact that this co-dependent woman lets him be self-absorbed, selfish, and just a plain jerk because, as a co-dependent woman, you lack confidence, self-esteem, and self-worth. But for us co-dependent women, we suffer in silence! All our wants, needs, and wishes are ignored and not necessary to these narcissistic men!

Anyway, this guy from one of my co-workers, who was supposed to be a man, had no job and dropped her off at work in her car (for which she paid). REALLY, girl! And payday, you would see all these women's men waiting for them to get off to get some money from them because it was payday. They are lined up in the parking lot. What a sight to see. This co-worker I was talking about was, of course, overweight. You have to be co-dependent because, number one, being overweight doesn't mean you're unattractive. You made that decision on your own. You have a choice either to lose weight, don't lose weight but represent yourself, and dress sexy and attractive, not frumpy and unattractive. But most of all, be bold and confident in your size, no matter how big you are. Am I helping someone who keeps attracting narcissistic, dysfunctional men? Just because you're overweight does not mean you are not beautiful or unattractive. Work on looking your BEST, no matter your size! White society now recognizes big girls and has big girl models like Ashley Graham and Tara Lynn, to name a few. We black women have been big all our lives, but now your plus size has models. What's that about? So, if they are big and beautiful, why can't YOU be too?

I was unhappy with my weight gain after my divorce and moved to Atlanta. I hired a trainer, lost fifty pounds, and kept it moving. It changed my life. I still have my trainer, around eight years, and I plan to keep him. He helps me stay motivated and in shape. What an incredible life transformation it was for me. I am no longer attracted to narcissistic men (maybe a few whom I kicked to the curb) but a lot of high-end men with money, jobs, looks, you name it. I married a good man, my soul mate. This you can do, too, if you get some help, counseling, and support, but it is a decision you must make on your own and stick to it. It got rough for me, but I stuck to it. Being in your fifties and dieting is not an easy task to do, but I was determined, and I did it! Do not let some tool guy take advantage of you. That is all I'm saying. You must dress for success! Stop buying all-black clothes that you think make you look smaller because often it does not, and it's a color that represents death; it's worn at funerals.

Instead, buy some bright colors like blue, orange, fuchsia, and red, my favorite color! I suggested to my co-worker that she lose some weight, get counseling, and get her self-worth and self-esteem back. But sadly, she did not take my advice! They seldom do! She is broken, TOO! For many of us, it is a lifelong struggle that gets the best of us. I am a survivor, and you can be too. Just put your foot down, get help from a professional counselor, and start your recovery journey! I can do all things through Christ who strengthens me Philippians 4:13.

Don't feel ashamed or embarrassed because I did precisely the same thing. I had low self-esteem and did not expect or receive anything but a tool man! You know you're broken when you accept little or nothing from a narcissistic man because real men have so much more than that to offer. I know this too, for I married a real man after counseling, Praise God! I now demand more than tools; you need respect, love, and, most importantly, God!" Oh, yeah, broke-ass men don't get it for me; you must have a JOB! I wish now some narcissistic man would ask me to move in with me or drive my car. He'd see what the back of me looks like as I turn and walk away! I changed, my perspective changed, too, and then my outlook did! I had no clue about my girl power that I had, none! I do now, and you can too! These damaged, toxic men don't have a steady job and are most likely to hustle for money (usually women). They don't work for the white man; at least, that was what my ex-husband used to tell me! And the kick part to this is you can be any color, black or white, rich or poor; it happens to any and everyone that is broken. And there are a lot of broken and dysfunctional people in this world, including me, all due to you got it, Satan!

Look at Britany Spears. She is so broken and dysfunctional that I feel her pain, yet she does not seek our creator of everything in existence; if she did, she would have her purpose in life. Again, she was given a talent and did not know what to do with it. The same happened in the Bible to the man who gave his servants skills according to their abilities. Long story short, the servant who hid his talent was taken from him and given to the servant who used his abilities. In other words, you lose it if you don't use it! God gives us purpose and direction, but we must seek Him (God) and not lean on our understanding. In ALL your ways, acknowledge him, and he will make straight YOUR PATH Proverbs 3:5. In other words, he will make your crooked path straight!

You allow these dysfunctional guys to do whatever to you because you have become a martyr; you can't help yourself due to childhood issues like rape, physical and mental abuse, and so forth; you get my drift! Again, we're BROKEN! The only thing you keep ending up with for your efforts are more kids and a wet ass! Yes, I said it. I'm trying to keep it 100%! That is precisely what happened to me. I had three kids and lots of wet assess! And I didn't enjoy sex due to childhood rape, abuse, and mistreatment for real. I'm trying to help somebody out there who has been in the Twilight Zone forever again, like me, broken and miserable! You can change your circumstances, but only YOU can decide!

I had never heard of this co-dependency condition because that is all it was, which wrecked my entire life. I've seen talk shows like Dr. Phil, Orpah, etc., but none on this subject. Did I happen to miss that show? It's because people refuse to address the big white elephant in the room or the ostrich with her head buried in the sand, get my drift. It's painful and hits home for many of us who are confused and whose life is in shambles. It's not really a bonified mental illness, but it's so close it's married to it because it affects your mind and your ability to think. You can't make adequate decisions because of your childhood traumas, your childhood living conditions (usually poor), abuse, and neglect, to name a few. All you want and need is for someone to love you, and the narcissistic man knows this and pretends to give it to you, but with a cost that you must pay! He hugs you and tells you all the right things to make you feel secure, only to take them away in his ongoing effort to control your life and MIND!

Again, this is partly because the Devil can see your future, and if you stay in faith, your blessings too. He isn't having that, so he sabotages your life so you will give up and lose your soul like many others who have even famous ones like Whitney Houston and her daughter Bobbi Christina; Joan Rivers, Anna Nicole Smith (she married a 90-year-old millionaire) so forth and so on. Whitney self-medicated, and Anna Nicole Smith did too with drugs and alcohol and killed themselves. What a waste of precious lives! Whitney was raised in the church; she knew the Lord; Anna Nicole was not into the church or God. Am I reaching anyone who, like me, had all those traumas happen to them too? That is why some of us throw in the towel, give up, and self-medicate with drugs, alcohol, crimes, prostitution, and so many other destructive behaviors I can't even name at this time! I felt that way, too, but God would not let me; he knew my struggles. He knew because Christ lived among us and suffered some of the same issues and now helps us to overcome ours! You must put your hands in the master's hand and lean not on your understanding! Call Him up and tell Him what you want. He never slumbers or sleeps Psalms 121:4. I read an article once with this caption: Good Morning, this is GOD; I'll be handling all your problems today and from now on! Did you get that?

After a nasty, painful divorce, I began domestic violence counseling with the help of family and friends. That's when I found out I was co-dependent. I was in denial; I did not believe the counselor. I asked him if co-dependency was an illness, sickness, mental illness, or what? He told me to look it up, and I did because, at first, it wasn't registering in my mind! I was in denial! So, I looked it up, and my face popped up on the screen, not literally, but it described me thoroughly! I was relieved, anxious, and angry (grieving stages), and at least I was not the only one with this condition that gave me some sort of comfort! Little comfort but still comfort. I felt I was too old to be going through these changes in my life; how could

I fix it simultaneously? I was in disbelief and denial about this new diagnosis of co-dependency, but reality set in, and I could finally see why I had the miserable, sorry life I was living! You know, as humans, when we have a traumatic experience, we go through five stages of grieving about it. Stay with me. I'm a nurse of forty-plus years; it's called the [Five Stages](). I see it every day in the life of a nurse, me! My patients are in poor health, have heart failure and kidney failure, and are on dialysis, and they all say the same thing, something like "l wish I knew this was going to happen," as they grieve about their situation. This is how a nurse discovered the grieving steps, and later, the medical field kept seeing this same pattern repeatedly in the patients, so much so they had to do something about it. Now, hospice, social workers, doctors, and nurses use it to assist patients in coping with their illnesses and deaths.

Stage 1, or the first stage of grieving, is called denial and isolation. People usually deny they have a problem or stop coming around. They just want to be left all alone so they can lick their wounds, sort of speaking. I've had patients go to the doctor, get a terminal illness diagnosis, and never return to the doctor until they get sick and are rushed to the hospital in an ambulance to die hours, days, or weeks later. What a waste of their life. Why they did not take care of their bodies is still a mystery to me.

Stage 2 of grieving is anger, usually with God. They say things like why did God let this happen to me because that is what I used to say. A lot of my patients got stuck in this stage. Some even died, still angry at GOD! They don't want to take responsibility for what they did or did not do to help them to treat their condition. Some even ignored it until it got worse and they got sicker. At one point, even I got tired of asking God why me because I kept repeating the same hurts, denials, and dysfunctions in my life! I felt that all my life, I went through drama and even let my circumstances get to me so much, so I gave up and stopped praying. You see, the Devil had strongholds on my mind; he had me. But when I read the Bible, it said Job lost everything; he had all his worldly possessions taken away but got it all back and more because he trusted God; the Bible says God lets it rain on the just as well as the unjust; that's why Psalms 73:2! Also, in Job 7:20, Job told his wife again shall we receive good at the hand of God and not evil? And sometimes, no words or rationalizations make sense to us to explain why we must endure hurting, pain, and suffering. But I can tell you this: it taught me to pray more and worry less. And I got all I lost: a house, a new car, and a new MAN!

I started to have more faith in God and myself. I kept saying you can do this; sometimes, you must talk to yourself to keep you motivated. Some people medicate, so I started praying more. I listened to gospels every morning on my way to work as well as at my desk at work. I read my bible and kept a miniature one in my purse. I read my Bible before I went to bed every night. I believed the word of God, and in about a year, my life turned around. I dreaded having to start over AGAIN, for the thousandth time, but I knew I could do it with God on my side. I relocated to Georgia, and the rest is history! Won't He Do It! Everything I lost in the divorce, I got back triple. A new home (my dad got for me on his Gl Bill), a new car, a black Mercedes, and a new man! No lies, it is true, and God has been opening the windows of heaven and pouring out my blessings, this being a big one since. I want to write a book so I can help someone over fifty get it together and transform their life like I did! I indeed have a testimony! Please buy my book and see how I transformed my life. You can, too, but you've got to be determined to do it!

I once saw this on a bumper sticker that read PUSH! As I approached the car, I could read what PUSH meant. It means to Pray about everything, every little bitty thing, and just be cool until He does His miracles. Sometimes, you have to wait until God works His magic (this process makes you grow patience), and last, it happens, so you push until something happens and keep moving! I also realized that I could only activate the blessings God had in store for me. You see, prayer activates faith, which activates your locked blessing. God unlocked the door, and after my divorce and counseling, I started receiving my blessing; praise God! My friends and family now tell me, look at your blessings, girl, you are doing it! And I am finally being rewarded for waiting patiently on God to replay all I lost for most of my life; praise God!

Stage 3 is grieving, in which people bargain again, usually with God; they say something like if my mother gets cured of, say, cancer, I'll never miss church or something equally as silly. They rarely do what they say they will do, but fewer people say stuff like this.

Stage 4 of grieving is depression; they don't want to see or hear from anyone. They just want to be left alone. Again, that was me so many times! People walk around like zombies without interacting with their environment, just breathing the air.

The final stage of grieving is Stage 5, when they finally get it together and accept the trauma, pain, and heartache and do something about it. God uses these situations in our lives to push us toward our purposes. Mine was now a mentor, author, educator, wife, mother, and grandmother. Again, God had plans for my life, plans of a future, and I began to claim them Jeremiah 29:11. He is a refuge and strength in ever-present help in trouble, Always! Psalms 46:1. I went in and out of relationships, enduring one bad one after another again all my adult life. My family tried to tell me something was wrong with me because I was in and out of these destructive relationships, but they did not know about my childhood traumas (alcoholic mother, physical and mental abuse, rape, etc.), they did not know my struggles of low self-esteem and self-worth. How could they know because I had no clue either? I just knew something was wrong, and I kept attracting and hooking up with these crazy-as-hell type men!

I went to my minister at the time after my first husband started physically abusing me for advice and comfort. He was much older, in his seventies. This was back in the early eighties. He told me that it was my duty as a Christian wife to stay with my unbelieving husband and pray about the abuse. Let me get this right: you are telling me to stay getting physically abused, beat up, black eyes, you name it, and wait on the LORD, I said to myself. I can't do that, I thought to myself. Well, needless to say, I did not take his advice again. I left this man and moved to Louisiana from California.

So, I got married again to another abuser worse than the first one. Damaged and dysfunctional people attract other damaged and dysfunctional people; we wear it on our faces, and body gestures all signal defeat and dysfunction. Our expressions are sad; we are depressed, angry, and sad. And narcissistic men look for that in their victims; you did get that, uh, I said victims, for that was exactly what I was at that time. You see, my husband at that time, in the early eighties, was raised by an abusive father who told him to beat his woman if they got out of line. That was what he did to my ex-husband's mother back then. And my husband back then was verbally, physically, and mentally abusive, jealous, lazy, and on crack drugs. So, when he became physically abusive, I left him. I was not going to stay in that situation. I'm not sure how that worked out for him, but I divorced him, too.

Again, I tried counseling with a minister who was supposed to be a counselor recommended by someone who had counseled him. I can't say whether it helped me or not either, but long story short, I ended up having an affair with the man. I was broken, and I just wanted love and affection from someone, anyone who could not hurt me anymore. Again, I was broken and in need of a real counselor who was experienced with domestic violence! So again, I tried to get some help. I just did not know what domestic counseling was at that time, and all this domestic violence was new to the public; there were no shelters back then in the eighties. Women were not protected and had few rights; we had just come from a period in the nineteen sixties where we could not vote or have credit in our name. We had few resources to turn to, and having counseling with a minister again at that time did not help me or my circumstances. This did not help me improve my self-esteem, nor did it make it worse! I felt terrible after the affair guilt because he was married; I felt like I was so unattractive. Again, wore glasses and short, žshort nappy hair; I wore wigs most of the time. I have suffered from poor self-esteem since childhood. I was teased for my glasses and bigger breasts by my peers. I had all sorts of hang-ups, which, again, came from childhood abuse and neglect. I had no clue of my importance or worth so far; I was miserable in relationships, which did not help my self-worth. If this sounds familiar like your life, now is the time to get some help and live the life you're supposed to live. The Devil has you fooled. If you think you can't get healed or do any better for yourself, you can! I am a witness and many, many others like me who have changed their lives!

I am in my sixties, yet I don't look or feel like I'm older because, get this right, I am not OLD! Maybe seasoned, but never OLD! God redeemed me and gave me a second chance to live and love. God is a God of second, third, and fourth; it doesn't matter how many times you mess up, he will always forgive you and assist you if you let him turn your life around! I will never ever look defeated and sad again in my life. God renewed me. You can't even tell I've been through so much in my lifetime; all I can say is, but GOD! Not only did the Lord heal me of co-dependency, but he sent me a good, REAL man, a Boaz man who loves me unconditionally; that is called icing on the cake! We travel all over, we go out on dates, and we enjoy each other. This can't get any better for me; thank you, Lord, like Etta James sang, "At Last, my love has come along! Won't God do it!!! Yes, he will!"

In co-dependency, you put other people's thoughts, needs, wants, desires, and feelings ahead of yours. You want to give other people what they need and want, BUT neglect yourself to do it. I was looking bad, overweight with glasses and a bad attitude. Plus, I was in the South, and prejudice was really bad. You were discriminated against in jobs, schools, and even restaurants. Get this: as a co-dependent woman, you plan your whole life around pleasing this man. You neglect all aspects of your life and ALL, and I do mean all other relationships, including FAMILY and your own kids, suffer because of this dependency. That right there tells me that we're sick when you neglect your own kids for some man!

What's up with that? Because you're broken.

My own mother neglected me and my brother for her boyfriends; we were already abused but even neglected when they came around. Mommy Dearest is a book about the child of an old famous actress, Joan Crawford, who was crazy as hell, probably schizophrenic (only someone with an addiction, she drank or mental illness) would abuse a child. Anyway, her daughter also wrote a book about her horrors and abuse at the hands of this actress. Well, my mother would make her look like a saint! My mother literally forgot about us when she had company. She would say something like 'Go play." We knew what that meant: get lost and not bother them. So, I took on the role of caring for my little brother, who was three years younger than me. I used to climb on a chair and cook for us when I was around five years of age.

When we got up in the morning if you woke up my mother, she would curse you out, so I started scrambling eggs and toast bread for our breakfast or putting cereals in a bowl for us. I still have a burn on my right forearm where I burned myself trying to cook us breakfast. I would make sandwiches for us for lunch. Sometimes, we had no meat, so I would fix mayonnaise or peanut butter and jelly sandwiches and powdered milk to drink. I HATE peanut butter today. I ate so much of it as a kid! Bread became our best friend; it kept us from being hungry. Sometimes, we ate just plain bread because that was all in the kitchen. If we were out of bread, we ate saltine crackers and drank Kool-Aid. This is what I'm talking about when I say neglect because that was what I endured as a child. There were no food stamps back then or WICC coupons; we got commode food from the government in silver cans, powdered and vegetables in a can. All the food was yucky, nasty, and tasteless. But we ate it because we were HUNGRY.

Your kids at five years of age should not have to cook for themselves or care for their siblings. I took on the role of a mother by caring for my little brother. I would get his clothes out and help him to get dressed for church and school, help him bathe himself, and remember he was three years younger than me. When I was five, he was just a baby at three years of age, so I took on the role of my mother! She was passed out and drunk in her bedroom, and you would catch hell if you woke "sleeping beauty!" This is the first time in my life I have told anyone about my childhood abuse. I, just like most trauma victims, kept it locked, rather buried in my mind way, way in the back(subconscious), because thinking about the horrors of my childhood is a source of anxiety, hurt, and pain for me! Writing about it offers me some sort of therapeutic (1 am emotional now) relief! Thank you 'all for your patience and understanding.

Our extreme dedication to a man damages all, and I do mean all, our relationships with our family, friends, and even our careers and jobs www.fortbehavorial.com. I divorced that abusive husband and married again another narcissus dysfunctional jackass. Oh, my bag, man; what was my problem? And he was the king of jackass; believe me, he was a work of art! I believed in the Bible, which said it was better to marry than burn in HELL Corinthians 7:9, so that was what I did.

We lived together seven years before I was foolish enough to marry him; I really thought that if I did not marry, I could lose my soul again. I was still broken and continued to wander in and out of broken relationships with broken, dysfunctional men. I was alienated from my kids; it almost destroyed my relationships because they could not stand the way he would talk to me, belittle me, or talk down to me like I was nothing. My husband lived in my house. I paid all the bills, and I helped him get up on his feet from drug addictions. He showed no appreciation and was arrogant and once said I was supposed to help him. He did not give me any money for household expenses and stated those are your kids, not mine. You take care of them, not me. I didn't make them! Yes, that is the jerk I was with for fourteen long, miserable years.

And I can't tell you why, except brokenness. I thought at first something was wrong with me. It was I was broken and kept attracting broken men. I prayed and prayed for God to fix him. All the while, it was me that needed fixing. I was co-dependent and broken and was in denial all the while I was in these dysfunctional relationships. My family hated him, as well as my friends; they kept trying to get me to leave, but I had tunnel vision; I could not see the forest for the trees. I was broken and needed a lot of help. I really thought that I could change him, LOL (laugh out loud)! But that didn't happen either. You can keep asking yourself why I get such stupid dysfunctional men, but until you get healed, YOU will never be able to answer that question. Like me, you can't see the forest for the trees.

Co-dependency is an emotional or psychological reliance on a man who usually needs support because he has an illness, usually a narcissistic personality disorder, alcoholism, or drug addiction www.oxford languages. To make you feel good about yourself, you neglect yourself and give others anything and everything they want and need because it validates you and helps you to feel confident, building up your self-worth and self-esteem helpguide.org. Also, as a co-dependent woman, you have no personal identity, interest, or value outside of your dysfunctional relationship and feel guilty about thinking or doing something for yourself. I would not buy myself any decent clothing at that time. I looked drab and dull, clean but plain and ordinary, looking nothing special about me. If I tried to dress up or fix my hair for church, my dysfunctional husband would make remarks like, "Who are you dressing up for the preacher? Are you fucking him too?" He was so ignorant it made me just pray more.

This is the kind of dysfunctional stuff I had to put up with. You see, dysfunctional men are really like scared children and so miserable and afraid you will leave them. Because hell, it's not love; they don't know how to do that! They don't want to lose out on the freebies you are affording them: house, car, food, etc. They like a woman who makes them feel powerful, competent and appreciated. After all, they're the shit, and you're not! They LOOK for women who are willing to sacrifice everything for them, and yes, there is some lonely and desperate woman who does just that. They look for these types of women to sacrifice it all for them and remain loyal to them, too. And we become stuck on stupid and this pattern of giving and sacrificing for them without the possibility of ever receiving anything back from their tired ass! Yes, I mean just that, which makes us angry, bitter, and depressed for not having the balls to confront this negro www.psychcentral.com.

These types of behaviors come from us sacrificing and giving of everything we have, which makes us even more pessimistic, and lower self-esteem issues, which manifest themselves into a learned behavior of helplessness that keeps us in these dysfunctional and toxic relationships. We think that if we put our men first, even before us, up on a pedestal, sort of speak, then they will show us affection and appreciation. I did! Unfortunately, they never do, which causes us to become irritated and frustrated, and yes, MAD! You really think you're doing something special for them. It makes you feel important, but not to them. They can care less because they have no real love, not less feelings for you. Get this co-dependency masquerade as LOVE! They do not Love YOU! Did you get that part about them not loving YOU? Because they don't, if they did, they would not abuse or mistreat you; it's a lie they tell you to keep you committed to them. Again, it makes me upset and angry why do we allow these assholes, my bag, these men to degrade and disrespect us? Okay, girls, you know why! We're broken and need some interventions. Yes, we need the Lord and counseling!

As co-dependent women, we get confused about love, relationships, and caring because we don't get any of that in relationships, and I will tell you why in the next chapter. I thought to myself, I had had enough of marriage once I got divorced, had counseling, and, for the first time in my life, got it all together mentally, physically, and financially. I used to say free at last, free at last, Thank You, Jesus, I'm free at last: I even had a freedom dance it's called the WHOBBLE! That dance came out when I got divorced, and I have been wobbling since, and very well, I might add!

God showed up and showed out for me, girls. He sent me Mr. Right, a REAL man! My prayers after my counseling and healing were to live happily and free for once without the need for toxic and dysfunctional men! And I did just that: I lived the single life and had a ball living it. My kids were grown up and had their own lives and families. I was truly free.

I got my own apartment and never went into the kitchen except to drink cold beverages, hardly cooked, and went out to eat every day (had dates). When I was home, I was naked as a jaybird kept my house clean (hardly ever) home. No one was there but me! I had lots of dates now because I had done a whole-body transformation, lost fifty pounds, and got my own personal trainer.

When I put my mind to something like this writing, I do whatever it takes to get it done. I hate procrastinators! At our age, whether you're going to do it or not. I'm too old to be waiting for something or someone's promises. I'll do it for myself. Get my drift? Anyway, I got physically toned and trim and was too hot to trot. You could not tell me anything! My cousin told me to sit my ass down now. You had too much fun, but not me. I was living the life I had only read about. I even received several proposals for marriage, but I said to myself, NEVER EVER AGAIN would I get married!

That's why I said, but God showed out he sent me my husband, a real man.

After several months of seeing each other, we knew we had something special; we found LOVE! Yes, it is real; you're missing out on real love, not the dysfunctional relationships I had all my life. Don't stay stuck on stupid; get you a real man girl like THE Lord sent me! I dated lots of guys; a few were dysfunctional, too. I dumped them. I refuse drama or dysfunction ever again, and so should you. Stop allowing these types of dysfunctional narcissistic men to hurt, shame, and abuse you. My grandmother used to say, "Men are like buses; they will come there, not going run out of them anytime soon!" So, keep looking because good men are out there. I have been with my husband now for seven years, and not once has he raised his voice or disrespected me NEVER! That is what love is. It does not ever seek to harm you. The Lord said in 1 Corinthians 13:1 that love is patient, love is kind, it does not envy, it does not boast, it is not proud, it is not rude, it is not self-seeking. It is not easily angered; it keeps no record of wrongs! If that does not sound like your relationship, then I'm sorry to say, but it's not LOVE! This truth will set you free because you need to know for yourself what love really is! I had read about it all of my life but never experienced it until now!

I began to know that my exes did not love me because of them and my kids. I did anything and everything for my exes but to no avail.

They still treated me like dirt and abused me physically and mentally, all because I was broken and had no self-esteem. I did not know I was co-dependent, and after fifty years of abuse all my adult life, it ended abruptly in a nasty divorce. I lost everything after fourteen years of anguish and had to start over in another state, Atlanta, Georgia, from Louisiana. Why? Because I was broken and finally got enough sense to go to therapy with a professional abuse counselor after my family and friends got involved. They had had enough of the abuse, and I finally did too!

One of the root causes of co-dependency is YOU! You're broken and suffer from low self-esteem, so doing for others helps fill your void. And these toxic dysfunctional predators look for this type of VICTIM, yes, victim, because their plan once they gain your trust is to use and destroy YOU!

As a broken individual, you do not feel worthy of love or happiness; I know I did not feel worthy. You feel like it's your job to keep other people happy. So, at that time, when I was married to my ex-husband, he wanted to buy all this stuff to make him look important to his family and friends again. I sold my home and bought a log cabin house with five acres of land, including horse stalls and fish pound with stocked fish. His family and friends were impressed and told him so, that really stroked his EGO! And I was looking stupid, not stupid but broken because I could not say no. Again, I was seeking some sort of appreciation, attention, love, something from this man I was stupid enough to marry. Not stupid, just broken and was filling a void! And whatever a narcissistic man asks, you cannot say NO to anything. Jump off a bridge, rob a bank, buy a log cabin with five acres of land, anything you agree to dumbly and blindly. I did that for my ex-husband. He wanted to own horses, so I sold my home in the city and moved to the area where you could own horses. We had two. The upkeep was costly, but he was happy because now he could brag to his family and friends about what he owned. He had no credit and couldn't buy a toothpick, not less a house and horses. I even helped him buy two trucks, in which he started his own trucking business boy. Was that a nightmare, another story, another time?

You hide all your thoughts, emotions, and feelings and even suppress them, causing you to feel resentful all the time. Yes, that was what I felt! That is why they call black women mad. We are being abused and taken advantage of by these toxic, dysfunctional, narcissistic men. And it spills over into every aspect of our lives, including work, church, school, and home. The kids become dysfunctional, too, because it's a vicious cycle, and the kids are raised in toxic, dysfunctional environments like mine. The daddy is abusive to them as well, cursing at them and even beating them. My mother was strict with us, whipping us with extension cords, switches, bats, shoes, and whatever she put her hands on. She was drunk most of the time, and it did not take much to set her off. My mother was also broken and wa also raised in a dysfunctional family environment too. My grandmother was an alcoholic, too, just not as abusive as my mother. And the vicious cycle continued with my brother and me.

My mother was an alcoholic, and she also smoked marijuana, which made her act up even more. I can't image how hard it must have been for her with two kids and a single parent on welfare. She also self-medicated with alcohol and drugs. She smoked cigarettes and died at forty from the cancer. She had some sort of personality disorder, too, I now see. She was also raised in a dysfunctional home, with her mother and my grandmother being an alcoholic. There was drama all the time in our house every stinky day. Once those two started to drink by evening, they were riled up and arguing and fighting and so forth and so on. This is what me and my baby brother had to put up with as kids. By the time I was twelve years old, I had had enough of the foolishness and could not take it anymore, so I ran away from the dysfunctional environment and went into a foster home. Meanwhile, the state got involved because after I ran away, my mom reported me missing, and I was picked up by the police. I was brought to juvenile and went to a court hearing, and the judge asked me why I ran away. I told her of the abuse, alcohol, and drugs and wanted to go live with my father, whom I never met and only heard of. And not good. Man, according to my mother. He never sent any money for our care, claimed my mother. I asked my father, who denied this. He claimed when he sent money, she would drink it up.

So, who knows what really went down because I could not figure out who was telling the truth?

'Long story short, my father came to California (where I was in a foster home) and got me, and I started my teenage years with my father, whom I had never seen in my life (that's another sad story for another time)! But I knew living with my mother was not working for me. I already was suffering with low self-esteem and no self-worth. You know something is wrong; you just don't know what it is exactly. You are not slow or stupid, but this is hard to figure out. Before I was told by my therapist that I was co-dependent, I had no clue. I never heard of it. No one talked about it. No talk show host, no preachers. In fact, no one did! Victims like me, who finally get out of the hurtful relationship, soon find themselves shortly in another one. It's because you are so used to the drama, neglect, abuse, and craziness, sad to say! It feels familiar to you because it is. You grew up with the same dramas you're experiencing with these guys.

We are broken, and without therapy, you wander in and out of these types of relationships because, again, you're broken and don't know that you are until you're in a hospital bed or in a shelter. Narcissi men are predators. They can smell your vulnerability; that is why we keep getting involved with them. They LOOK for women who lack self-esteem and self-worth psychcentral.com. They will pass up a normal, healthy woman for a broken one. A woman who knows who she is won't tolerate these disrespectful, toxic guys, while a broken woman will. There is no way now I'd have a man of mine living with my number one, no job, broke number 2, and then physically and mentally abuse me! Hell, to the NO! So, if it looks like a duck and has feathers and quicks, then it's a duck; in other words, it's you, and you are broken. You cannot keep avoiding the truth; get help! You need help, and no one is going to help you get the help you need, especially the other people you've been keeping happy while you are miserable. They are too busy being happy and content while you kill yourself, making them happy. I'm trying to help a sister out like me who could not figure out how to climb out of a paper bag, not less how not to get involved with narcissistic men!

You see, narcissistic men are charming and attentive at FIRST; once your defenses drop, they come in for the KILL! Co-dependent people like you and me feel like we will never find a good man (that's a stronghold the devil plants in our minds). The Devil is a liar and the father of liars John 8:44. So instead of being alone, we hook up with a no-good narcissistic man, not good!

You see, because we expect feelings of being loved stemming from childhood, we fear being alone. So, we play the role of the martyr who is loyal, devoted, and patient with this asshole, my bag this. We hear bells and see red flags, but we ignore them out of ignorance. Again, we're broken and don't know that until we get help!

The relationship is one-sided. You're doing all the work. Something is wrong with them as well; they have psychotic and narcissistic personality disorder. Yes, it is a real diagnosis, and yes, they are just CRAZY! They have no remorse or no bad feelings for treating others like dirt. How do you not have feelings after you physically abuse someone? It's called Crazy and some sort of personality disorder, narcissism, more than likely. At first, you think, what's wrong with this dude, and then after a while, he convinces you that you're the crazy one and he's not. They flip the script in a minute and do the Dr. Jackal/Mr. Hide routine and will lie at the drop of a hat. I was reading this article about a woman who was living with her narcissistic boyfriend. This woman, who was in a narcissistic relationship, was convinced by this man that she was crazy, and she went to a psychiatrist for a session. In the end, the psychiatrist told her there was nothing wrong with her. How about that! That is how convincing a narcissist's man can be. They can make you doubt yourself!

There are several causes of co-dependency, but the root cause of co-dependency for me was my childhood. It was horrible, and my mother was on a trip, to say the least. We had no Christmas, birthdays or holidays, no vacations, nothing. Every dollar she got hold of went to alcohol and drugs. She was an addict and could not help herself. After I grew up, I could understand addiction, but not as a child. Anyway, co-dependency usually starts in the first five years of your life. I was raised poor in the hood, or ghetto, as we used to call it. I suffered from abuse from my mother and her alcoholism and drug use. I was afraid of her, and if she gave you that look or stare, you knew she was going to give it to you when you got home, which was a beating. And back then, you could not call the cops for getting an ass beating. It was not considered child abuse and was not against the law!

Co-dependency usually happens in a home where the children's needs, wants, and emotions are ignored or punished issues. This emotional neglect and abuse can contribute greatly to a child having low self-esteem; after all, they are ignored and made to feel unimportant to the person who matters the most to them, the mother or father. The child will begin to feel like they are not worthy of anything and, thus, of unimportance to their family. So, you see, co-dependency is born out of a household of abuse, neglect, addiction, and alcoholism, which is where I developed my co-dependency. Also suffered from trauma. I was abducted and raped by a friend's family member, so that also contributed to my co-dependency. No wonder all my adult life was horrible. I was severely broken! But God had a plan for my life, for he said, I have a future for you Jeremiah 29:11. God said for I know the plans I have for you, plans to prosper you and not to harm you, plans to give you hope and a future! I believe in the word of God, for God does not ever lie. Why would he? After all, he created us. He did not promise us milk and honey and good times all our lives, but he did promise to be with us always and never leave us Deuteronomy 31:6.

You may ask why God allows these types of occurrences to happen to us. Life happens to the rich, poor, smart, and mentally challenged. The Devil is trying to steal your soul like he tried with Job in the Old Testament. God allowed the Devil to take everything from him but his life. The Devil was hoping Job would curse God and die, but he did not. Job got it; he said to his wife when God sends good things, we accept them, so how can we complain when he sends trouble? Job never said anything against God! Job 2:10. So how can we complain? It is life. Mayo Angelo once stated after she was raped as a child, too, you must go out and kick ass even after trials come. Because you will be faced with trials and tribulations until you die, and not just you but any living individual will, too. The difference is how YOU choose to handle it and let it destroy you, so you get addicted to drugs or the way I do with prayer and waiting on God! Prayers of the righteous man are powerful and effective James 5:16. Oprah Winfrey once said that the only courage anyone ever needs is the courage to follow your own DREAM and love yourself, and have the courage to follow your passion. You've got to figure that one out on your own!

You've got to believe in the word of God and the POWER he possesses. You see, I learned my love of God from my great-grandmother, who took me and my brother to church rainy, cold, hot, sick, you name it, we never missed church. I thank God she did that for me. I didn't realize that the Devil was so 'powerful, but he is. He roams around the earth, looking for someone to devour. Remember, his only reign is on earth Peter 5:8. When God comes back, he will chain Satin forever, and the Devil is not going peacefully; he is taking as many souls as he can to HELL with him. After all, an old and true saying is misery loves company.

Yes, the Devil is already busy using sex to drive souls to HELL with him. Look at the TV: sex is everywhere, as well as homosexuality, women on the pole that's a big thing now, tattoos on the bodies of young people. Now drugs are legal like Marijuana, all that is designed by the Devil to get you to curse God and lose your soul. Now, young people are living together. I had a co-worker and her eighteen-year-old daughter, who graduated from high school and moved in with her boyfriend; how insane is that? As a mother with three daughters, I did not allow them to date until they were sixteen or seventeen years old, but shacking with a boy absolutely NOT! I had expectations for them, and they knew it. I sent them to college to get their education so they would not have to rely on a MAN! And I am proud to say they are all independent black woman and do not have abusive relationships; praise GOD!

Forgive me, but the Holy Spirit took me there, so for co-dependent adult women, childhood trauma is often another root cause of co-dependency. The co-dependent relationships are often a response to unaddressed past childhood traumas such as rape, incest, alcohol, drugs, physical and mental abuses, divorce, and domestic violence www.brightquest.com>blog. Yes, I dealt with all of these occurrences as a child, which explains why I messed up all my life. As I mentioned earlier, I was abducted and raped as a teenager; my first sexual act was being raped! You don't think that shit messed with my head; well it did!

I saw my mother and grandmother fighting other people. I saw neighbors fighting, usually, men beating up their wives or girlfriends. We lived in an apartment complex, and one Saturday night, I heard the neighbor hollering and screaming for help. My mother, myself, and my little brother ran next door, and the neighbor was in the bathtub, and her boyfriend was punching her in the face. Her eyes were bloody, swollen shut and closed, and he was beating her with his fists. My mother called the police, and when they arrived, he was arrested. Several days later, I saw him with the woman; both her eyes were black, and he was back in her apartment. I see now she was co-dependent, and he was a narcissi jackass, my bag man. If a man hits or harms you physically, mentally, or verbally, he is not a man, and HE does not love Y O U! This woman, next door to us was a broken, poor woman, and he was toxic and dysfunctional, to say the least. Am I helping someone? Has anyone who has been there also done that? Again, co-dependency is not LOVE! It is a love addiction that can and will destroy you as a person as well as the relationship. Again, the girl's co-dependency masquerades as LOVE! Don't fall for it; get some help and get out of that toxic, one-sided merry-go because that is all it is.

Another fact about co-dependency is that it can be a learned behavior passed down from one generation to the next, which happened to me. My mother got it from her mother's co-dependency and passed it on to me. My mother never told my baby brother that she loved us or me; we were in a loveless relationship with her; again, she was broken, and I really feel she had some underlying personality disorder as well. When she drank, she turned into Dr. Jackal/Mr. Hyde became verbally as well as physically abusive. She got mad at me one time and called me a "stupid bitch" and kicked me in the stomach. I remember the pain in my stomach was so great I was doubled over in pain and crawled to the room and into my bed and cried myself to sleep while I prayed for the Lord to remove me from this situation. That is when I made up my mind to run away. But after therapy, I stopped that cycle, and so far, my kids are in healthy relationships. I hope and pray for any woman who finds herself in a co-dependent relationship to get help. Trust me. You cannot change without the help of a—counselor or psychiatrist. I tried to no avail; I still attracted dysfunctional men! You see, I had extremely low self-esteem and felt a void. I felt empty inside unless I was taking care of someone. Again, I was a broken woman!

Co-dependency is like a vicious cycle, a circular relationship and a cycle of co-dependency causing you to have further low self-esteem and low self-worth, which comes from you sacrificing yourself for this man who is happy to receive your sacrifices," What to know about co-dependent relationships" T. Legg, J. Berry 10-13-2017. Co-dependency often includes emotional, physical, and verbal abuse, making you feel worthless. The men get satisfaction from knowing you're taking care of all their needs and wishes. You really think as co-dependent that these men need you, which gives you a purpose. We stay in those relationships even when the man is abusing us because he brings us flowers or half ass apologizes for his anger. You have difficulty making decisions while you are in this so-called one-sided relationship. After all, you are co-dependent and cannot function on your own.

And these guys get that! That's why they LOOK for us, broken women!

You literally built your whole world around this sucker, destroying all other relationships; that's how you know you are co-dependent and broken. You cannot see the forest for the trees because, again, you're so broken and need some type of intervention. Your family, kids, and friends all can see that you're in a destructive relationship, but because of your tunnel vision of help, I know because that is what I did.

When I was getting married to my kid's father, we got married at the house, and while I was getting dressed, my two cousins, who were my bridesmaid, actually opened the window up and tried to get me to climb through and not marry a dysfunctional psychotic jackass again, I mean man. They were trying to rescue me from myself and another miserable life with this dysfunctional man.

He was physically and verbally abusive and was doing crack at that time. I don't know today why I married him because I did not love him. I think I was trying to give my kids a father in the home because my father was not in our home growing up. But again, I was broken and could not see the light, so I went through another dark hole with him as well. My family tried and tried but to no avail. I kept attracting dysfunctional men because, again, dysfunction attracts dysfunction, and predators seek an esteemed woman to dominate and control like me at that time. Please, again, if you're broken and that sounds like your life, get help and stop the insanity!

Chapter 2 Why Do I Keep Hooking Up with Toxic Narcissi Men?

First, we need to understand exactly what a narcissistic man is. I'll say it again and again: you can't do better unless you know (educated) better! This chapter tries to describe some of the behaviors and traits of the narcissistic man. There is not one description, but most of the time, some of these men have similar traits of each of the four categories (grandiose, covert, communal, and malignant) and use various tactics but will mention just gas lighting in this chapter, which I found appalling. I'm just overwhelmed after writing this chapter and appreciative of God that I am finally free of the narcissistic monster I was with for so long. Monsters, bogymen, they still exist, except now they walk among us and are called toxic, dysfunctional, psychotic, or narcissistic, to name a few! The Bible says in my favorite Bible verse not to be afraid, yea though I walk in the valley of death, I will fear no evil for thy art with me 1 Psalm 23:4. God knew this, so it is no surprise to him that is why you trust and depend on him. All I can say is trust God and hold on to his unchanging hand in these times we're living in. And I'm glad now we can put a name on these monsters, and again, it's called the Devil, and he has crafted some very sick individuals; just be careful. The Bible says that the Darkness (Devil) cannot overcome the light (God), John 1:5.

We hear the term all the time: he's a jerk or narcissist, but what is a narcissi's man? Let me clear up myths with facts. First, narcissistic men are crazy. Yes, they have an underlying mental condition called NPD (Narcistic Personality Disorder) mayoclinic.org. They test some of the craziest, sickest people who appear to have narcissistic symptoms, which a licensed psychologist performs. That's how they know about these types of men. They perform these tests in prisons, jails, or doctor's offices so they can study these personality disorders. This is where most of these crazy people are housed. They usually get caught committing some of the most hideous crimes and get caught and incarcerated.

I recall in Louisiana, this narcissistic man committed a crime; this woman met the man in a bar, brought him home, and had sex that night. In the morning, when she woke up, he had beheaded her autistic son's head; I'm not making this up. He was sitting at the table eating, and her son's body was lying on the floor beside his head. It is a miracle he didn't kill her, too. You must be careful; you don't know what you'll pick up in the streets. Again, they are predators; they literally do it for a living. Looking for innocent, unknowing individuals like you and me to pick up. Everything that glitters is not GOLD! It's an old but true saying.

And get this: these narcissistic men make up 80% of the population, and only 20% of women have this type of personality disorder. That's why we keep hooking up with them. There are a lot of them buggers roaming around looking for the US! They're everywhere: work, school, church, nightclubs, gyms, concerts, you name it, they're everywhere that women hang out. I even see them now at the nail salon getting pedicures and manicures! What man do you know who gets pedicures? I never knew not one of these dudes. They're charming, usually good-looking, looking well dressed, and seem to have some sort of money or credit cards. Now, whose name is on credit cards is another matter because it may not be their name but one of his conquests!

I dated a narcissistic man who was a civil engineer before I married my husband. His name was not on his car registration, and when I asked about it, he said it was an old girlfriend (Red Flag) who bought him this car. He was charming, had credit cards, and wore designer clothes, but he still was crazy; he wanted to know where I was and what I was doing, etc., all the franken time you get the picture!' Girl, he was trying to keep up with me for real. He would pass by my apartment to see if my car was there. One night, I was out with another friend and did not get home till late in the morning. He kept texting and calling me, so I cut my phone off! Long story short, after several months, I ended this foolishness and broke it off, blocking his number in my phone.

This reminds me of a story about this woman who was out hiking in the woods and came upon a snake that looked like it was dying (red flag). So, you picked it up, brought the snake home, and nursed it back to health. She thought this snake would be grateful to her for saving his life. One day after she fed the snake, he had gotten better; she was giving the snake some water, then he bit her. She began to get sick, and she looked at the snake and asked him why he would do that to her. He replied with that long fork-looking tongue hissing, "'cause I'm a snake, and you knew that when you brought me home with you, you should have left me in the woods!"

How's that for gratitude? But the snake was absolutely right. Get the POINT? Leave those dysfunctional men alone; wait upon the Lord for a good man! The morale of that story is to leave these sick individuals where you me them! I am very cautious when I'm out and meet a guy. Forest Gump said that life is like a box of chocolates; you don't know what you will pick!

I've heard stories, and I know you have, too, from guys who were involved with narcissistic women, too. One guy told me his narcissistic girlfriend cut him with a knife while arguing over food. Another guy told me that he was involved with a narcissistic woman who cut him with a knife in his side because he told her he did not want to see her anymore because of her behavior. These types of people are really sick mentally and need help. Usually, narcissistic men do not seek treatment because we all know that men refuse to get therapy. After all, they feel it is a weakness; it is not; it's smart!

These narcissistic men display symptoms of some mental condition, such as difficulty regulating emotions and behaviors, and experience major problems dealing with stress and change wwwmayoclinic.org. And the major symptom narcissistic men show is a lack of empathy and an inflated sense of their self-importance. They need EXCESSIVE attention and admiration, always have troubled relationships, and take advantage of people to get what they want. Does that sound familiar to anyone, and is this not a red flag? If you're in a relationship and all you do is argue, fuss, and fight like I did, then more than likely, he is narcissistic, psychotic, and dysfunctional; let's be real about it! Again, if it walks like a duck, has feathers and quakes, it's a duck. In other words, he's CRAZY! I bet you know someone who has been or currently is in a relationship with a narcissistic man. I know plenty of woman like me who had low self-esteem or was broken and kept getting into relationships with narcissistic men. Why? Good question, and I'll try to answer it in this chapter. Again, you can't do better unless you know better!

These narcissistic, toxic, and crazy men look for; I said they look for certain types of women like old rich ladies, low self-esteem ladies, overweight ladies, lonely ladies, unattractive, plain, and even ugly women who are in a vulnerable place in their lives.

When I was single and went out alone, many younger guys always came on to me. I was in my fifties (but didn't look like that) and still don't look my age now. When they would approach me, I'd smile first. I didn't need their money (I had my own independent black woman that I am), refused their drink (have one, thank you), and asked them, "What can I do for YOU!" Now, most of them just wanted to hook up for fun and games, get my drift? I declined and kept it moving and next!

After going out with several guys, two had the nerve to ask me to co-sign for a new car! I looked crazy at them and asked them to repeat what they just said! Because I know you did not ask me to co-sign for someone, I don't know a car. Yes, they did; narcissistic, dysfunctional men will do just that, no feelings or emotions, just looking for someone broken to buy them a car and ruin her credit. Again, I declined and kicked them to the curb, NEXT!

Now I know someone who did give her man a used car, her daughter's car. She was behind for three months in her car notes and was in college, so my friend took her daughter's car and gave it to her man. That relationship didn't last three months, and she damaged her relationship with her child over that jackass! Yes, éhe did. She was broken, too, and kept going in and out of broken relationships, just like me. The difference was I got help, and she did not; in fact, she is still doing it, hooking up with dysfunction men. I promise you I'm not making any of this stuff up; it really happened! If you're just coming out of a difficult and painful marriage or break up, then these men are predators, and they can sense this and thus, will target you.

Now I'm not being funny, so don't get offended, but if you're unattractive and fat and a good-looking guy starts to come on to you and starts flirting with you and giving you a lot of complements and attention, that to me that right there is a huge RED FLAG! I'm not saying a nice guy won't talk to you, but a fine, well-dressed woman would be a RED FLAG! I'm just trying to be real with you. You should be careful. There are a lot of mentally challenged people out here, and some are looking for a sugar mama to finance and support them and their egos! If this is you, stop the insanity, get counseling, and get some much-needed help! Again, there is nothing wrong with being alone. Before I married, I went to shows and out to eat alone. I started hobbies and dance classes, etc., to keep me busy.

Church, Bible classes, there are so many things to do besides having a crazy ass man to have to deal with. I'd rather be alone and pray about it. My prayer was to be single, healthy, and happy, and that was what I was. But low and behold, God sent me my good and faithful Boaz man. Praise the Lord!

I had a coworker who was a single nurse. She was overweight, so she would order pizzas on the weekends she was off. Well, this fine and attractive-looking pizza driver came on to her, and they started sleeping together. After several months of them not going out anywhere (red flag) and only staying in her home, she asked him why. He told her he was only sleeping with her and he was not going to introduce her to his family and friends. He was just having sex with her, and that was all it was to him; he also mentioned she was overweight and not the kind of woman he usually dated. What a jerk, narcissistic asshole. She was hurt and stopped ordering pizza from that place and never saw him again; he only wanted to have sex with her. She was lonely, overweight, with poor self-esteem, he knew that, and because of her loneliness, she allowed him to just be a botty call! Come on, girls, don't fall for the okay dope. If you are overweight and tired of being alone, do something about it like I did. I hired a trainer and began my transformation, and you can too. Purchase my book and start your transformation today, and do not leave counseling and God out!

We wear our hurts, sorrows, pains, and losses on our faces, posture, and attitude. That is how narcissistic men know so much about you because that was exactly what I did when I met my narcissistic ex-husband. I had depression and was sad all the time and angry again.

I was broken and desperately needed some therapy. My codependency was a lifelong struggle that often left me depressed, sad, and angry. Anger at my mother, father, life, and circumstances, mostly the dysfunctional men I kept hooking up with. Co-dependent and narcissistic men develop complementary roles that fill each other's needs. A co-dependent woman found a man she could pour herself into, and he found a woman who would put his needs before hers. Selfish, narcissistic men are incapable of loving other people. They're only capable of not loving THEMSELVES! As his ego grows and grows, so does his demands until the co-dependent woman eventually burns out; that is what happened to me. I got so burned out after fourteen years of sacrificing myself for my ex-husband I just could not do it anymore. I didn't want to. I was exhausted. And they are NEVER EVER satisfied; they keep asking for more! With narcissistic men and co-dependent woman, even when the relationship turns abusive, the woman still stay as I did for fear of being alone! Is that silly or what? Not when you're broken; it makes perfect sense to you! Anyway, these men. Will pick you out of a crowd and heap on lots of extraordinary complements and ask all sorts of personal questions like are you married, have any kids, your occupation (big one), live alone, etc., so they can PLOT not PLAN how to gain control of you, your life and most of all your moulay aka money! These types of guys go in and out of relationships because, remember, they must have ALL the control. Some women will not tolerate it, obese, ugly, or whatever, and I applaud them. Good men and LOVE are waiting on you, but you must believe in God to claim your blessing, aka a good man like I now have. LOVE is the most POWERFUL thing on earth, more powerful than hate. Hate can turn into LOVE. That's how powerful real love is.

Dysfunctional men, like the narcissistic ones, keep you down because it makes them feel good. It boosts their "EGO!" I once worked for a lady doing home health, and she had four businesses. She was overweight, about five hundred pounds, and could hardly walk. She waddled like a duck she was big but short about five feet. I am not making this up. It is true. She loved to eat. In fact, that's all she did. So, one day, we were at work, and her son-in-law came in with a much younger guy than she was (about twenty years younger). She was in her fifties, and this guy was in his mid to late thirties. Long story short, the guy started taking this woman out on dates in three months, and he moved in with her. Now, for me, this would be a RED FLAG! But obviously, loneliness is a mother, and so is low self-esteem. Now again, 'if I was fat, let's call an ace an ace, and all I did was eat, wouldn't you question a man coming on to you at your job? I'm sure her son-in-law bragged to this guy about her businesses, her money, and her being by herself. I feel like the son-in-law helped set her up! He helped this guy steal her money and ruined her business.

I also worked for another woman with a home health business and married her boyfriend. Sad to say, he did the same thing to her. She had a huge wedding with a custom-designed white wedding gown and a beautiful reception I attended with some of the other workers and about three hundred guests. She was in her forties, and her husband was also in his thirties; I wondered what was really happening. Am I not the only woman, or are they broken too? Because. These marriages were dysfunctional, and neither lasted. After these guys went through their money, they split! Left them high and dry without any money; the last I heard, one of the ladies was working in a hospital as a nursing assistant. I think that was her profession before she started her home health business.

This is what a narcissistic man does. First, he targets you; he already had in his mind to go after this woman (my boss, who was obese and walked like a duck, no lie) because he knew she was alone and vulnerable (he got that information from the son-in-law). His next move was to flatter: flirt and perform so convincingly she wouldn't know what he was up to. Last, gain her confidence, then go in for the KILL! Now, if you're in doubt about someone, first do what I did. After we seemed to become serious about our relationship, I took my husband to meet my close family and friends. Your family and friends will tell you what they see in your man upfront! So, I took my then-boyfriend, now my husband, to meet my family in Dallas, Chicago, and Louisiana, and not one person, not one, had a negative comment about him. In fact, they loved him and told me how great a guy he was. That made me feel relieved because I had married a narcissistic jackass who treated me like shit! After my therapy, I was careful about who I dated or went out with. Obviously, age has nothing to do with it; this lady (who was obese and walked like a duck) was in her fifties. You would think she knew better, but she did not. Again, she suffered from codependency; I bet you any amount of money, low self-worth, and her weighing five hundred or more pounds didn't help her self-esteem either. She clearly had an eating disorder because that was all she did.

You have to be careful out here now that 80% of the population are narcissistic men. If this guy you meet is charming, please you with many compliments for me; this is a RED FLAG! In six months, this lady I was talking (an obese one that walked like a duck) about went to Las Vegas and married this young boyfriend, RED FLAG! He then took over the financial side of her four businesses. Red flag, Damn! Her adult kids, who also worked in her businesses, were upset by this time and tried to talk to her, but to no avail. She thought he really loved her, poor thing! Red Flag! Sometimes, a heart wants what it wants! He bought her roses to work every day, a new color of roses, he took her out to eat in fancy restaurants, oh he really piled on the goodness and kindness like honey, another RED FLAG! I know she had that gut feeling something was wrong; this man was rushing her into this romantic relationship. But she ignored it and threw caution to the wind (old but true saying)! Apparently, she was not ever used to this sort of attention and faked yes; I said it was fake affection. Suddenly, our paychecks started bouncing all around like a basketball. We had to wait a month before she could pay us.

I saw the handwriting on the wall and the other people working for her. We started looking for another job; we were not buying what he was trying to sell! I had three kids. I quit and found another job but later heard he stole all her money, and she lost all her businesses. He was a predator, and she had no self-esteem and was lonely, and he came in for the KILL! He wiped out her bank account, cars, jewelry, you name it, and she did not sign a prenup either. I felt her pain, but she should have known, shouldn't she? Apparently, being lonely is a mother; I must say it will cause you to not think but react badly for some. Trust your intuition, your gut, sirens, bells, whistles, or red flags, for that is the only thing that they cannot control in narcissistic men! But, like me, you can choose to ignore them. I did, but I was broken and did not know any better. I know better now!

I also have coworkers who do online dating. Don't you think these men aren't narcissistic, too? Yes, they target lonely women and scam them; it happened to one of my coworkers as well. She was a lonely, overweight, single parent who did online dating. Long story short, she got catfished and sent a man five hundred dollars to come visit her. RED FLAG! What the HELL! You got it; he took her money, and she never heard from him again. She was broken, lonely, and needed help, but she refused TO GET HELP. She thinks she's okay, but again, everyone will not get help and change. I did, and my life was transformed. Praise the Lord! Some ot you may wonder what causes these narcissistic men to be so cruel, selfish, and toxic and why they are so evil. Well, Dr Ramani Durvusula, in her YouTube series, says their home environment and circumstances make these guys. Again, narcissistic men are not born but are made by their environment. It is a CHOICE. Let me break it down even further for you to really understand what is happening. It is rooted in self-loathing and low self-esteem, usually from some sort of trauma like rape or physical abuse.

Yes, again, our childhood does shape our life as an adult. If you are damaged from trauma in your childhood as an adult, you must fix it; it's called therapy; otherwise, you will NEVER heal; you cannot do it alone; you are going to need some professional help! These guys, as boys, had chaos, trauma, neglect, spoiling, codependence, alcohol, and drugs in their environment as they were growing up. By the time they reach their twenties, a narcissistic personality emerges. After all, it comes from all the negative circumstances in their life. They like to hook up with co-dependent women because they have similar childhood traumas; they just adopt and cope with them differently. Because of the traumas, these men formed a fractured sense of self. These men choose the evil component in their lives. In life, everyone has choices. Two forces exist in this world: good (God) and Evil (Devil).

There are two pathways or roads for you to travel. One leads to destruction, evil, death, and life in HELL! The other pathway is toward the Lord. You love people, help people, do good to people, and live a healthy, productive life; for it, you go to an eternal home in heaven. Your CHOICE John 14:6. Now the Devil shows you money, fame, women, and wealth; all you must do is act like an ass (narcissistic) to get everything you want. You step all over people, commit crimes, steal, rape, you name it for the Devil. You are so caught up in the lifestyle on your deathbed bed you forget, die, and go to your eternal home in HELL!

Or you can be humble, love God, love your family and friends, and show love and compassion for everyone, die and live forever with the CREATOR! It doesn't take a rocket scientist to choose the right way, but often Satan blinds people so much so they can't see just what he is setting them up for, which is failure. He speaks to their minds telling them there's nothing wrong with taking this or that the store won't miss it or raping a woman she wanted it anyway. Can you feel where I'm coming from? There is no cure for narcissism, but there is treatment, which is psychotherapy and counseling for codependency issues. But sad to say, few seek out therapy. It's called PROUD! I know because I have nursed for forty-plus years, and I have been on the deathbed of many people who had that regret of not seeking God and his kingdom and were afraid to die. They already knew what awaited them: death and a burning hell forever! There is always a PRICE you have to pay for your choices in life.

I once had a friend who dated a drug dealer. The money cars he drove amazed her so much that she slept with him and had a relationship with him. He bought her a new car and jewelry and gave her lots of money. She got her nails and hair and had designer clothes, shoes, and purses. Well, he went to jail and got a life sentence back in 80's it was a life sentence to sell drugs. She stated that she was getting sick, couldn't eat, and was losing weight. Went to the ER one night; she was in so much pain. They did blood work, found she was HIV positive, and admitted her for treatment. Long story short, she died several years later. Last I heard, he was still in prison. She lost her life and soul over some bull; it's called the love of money!

The Bible says, it profits a man to gain the whole wide world and LOSE his soul. Mark 8:34.

Look at all the famous abusive people like James Brown. His daughter Yamma Brown wrote a book about his abuse of them and their mother. David Ruffin was also abusive and damaged. He was narcissistic, as well as Tom Cruise, Justin Bieber, Donald Trump (we knew he was crazy), Drake, O.J. Simpson (he clearly acted crazy), and the biggest one, Adolph Hitler (he killed all those Jews because he believed in a pure white race of people but not the Jews, he was truly crazy)! And that is not all of them; it can happen to anyone and everyone who has suffered trauma or addictions from unhealthy environments in their childhood! Also, some serial killers are narcissistic; they lack empathy, have no sense of accountability, and are usually grandiose.

To help you out with something else about narcissistic men, they have four types. Yes, these buggers are really crazy but can be smart, manipulative, and calculating, so be careful when dealing with them but be informed like I'm trying to tell you. The types of narcissistic men are grandiose, malignant, convert, and communal. Boy, are they mixed up, confused, and again, just plain crazy, so tell me why you're in a marriage or relationship with them? All these narcissistic men use SEX as a pawn to get to you!

YES, I said they use sex as a pawn in this game because that is all you are to them, and sex is a way of getting what they want from you. And these men are usually good lovers and skillful in lovemaking, get my drift? That is why you do not sleep with a guy after several dates; if that is all he wants, then if you don't give it to him, he will not stay. He will ghost you, no calls, no texts, etc. Good riddance; it will save you from heartaches and pains, trust me. Never give your goods (sex) to an unworthy man; wait on God. Some women, out of brokenness, offer their bodies to these types of damaged men who use this to control them and their money, get a free house to live in, drive a car around, and screw for free. Last I heard, gas isn't cheap, groceries aren't either, so why are you allowing some man to use and abuse you?

Again, we're broken and need counseling! Some of you have a purpose for your life, like me. I had no clue! I was broken all my adult life, but after an ugly divorce and counseling, I found my direction and purpose in my life. God renewed me. Do I look broken now? Hell No! He did it for me and will do it for you; that's the kind of God I serve! You can achieve any little bitty dream. The power is in your precious hands! Who knew I would be writing a book? Me, a co-dependent, abused, former rape victim, who? Not me. All I can say is, but GOD! He can and will do what man cannot do!

To start, the first crazy, I mean the type of narcissistic man is the grandiose narcissistic man-boy, is he dozy! They are usually in high-profile positions like CEO of business, Chiefs, Head or Secretary of a Department, and even Presidents, which recalls ex-president D. Trump and V. Putin these two are classic examples of grandiose narcissistic men. These men are really sick; this grandiose narcissistic disorder is a bonified REAL mental illness disorder and is described in the Diagnostic Statistical Manual of Mental Disorders Manuel under Narcissistic Personality Disorders. They are ever so charming like syrup, sweet, attentive, attention seeking extravert. Now, an extroverted personality is sociable, talkative, assertive, and excitable. These guys seek out social stimulation and opportunities to engage with people.

Grandiose narcissistic men are vane, bold, obnoxious, and shameless, much like Ex-President D. Trump. Does this not describe him or what? They tend to be self-absorbed, entitled, callous, exploitative, authoritative, and aggressive. Some are even physically abusive (they will physically harm you when angered or mad), unempathetic (your mother died, so what they would say: something like that), callous, think highly of themselves (I'm your master either you do as I say, or I will kick your ass, say something like that).

Now, on the other hand, they have high self-esteem while they continue to downgrade you and your self-esteem; they are satisfied with their life (despite the pain they inflict on you) due mostly to you sacrificing your happiness, life, and love unto their ungrateful asses! They must show outward acclaim, attention, and domination. They have to be all that in public or at home. They're the boss and won't ever let you forget it! They don't have relationship skills; it's all one-sided you are always doing for them. That's how you know you're in a dysfunctional relationship. And they love making you miserable and unhappy!

Does this sound like the kind of man you want to have in your life, yet we do? We fall in love because he gives you great sex; he has it going on in that department. It's the best sex you've ever had. But did you know they use it as power over you to get you to do whatever they want you to? Red Flag, Red Flag! Not good girls, get rid of him and wait on the guy God will send you like I did.

God knows your wants and needs, but we're too impatient, lonely, and won't wait for the Lord. God works in his time frame, not ours. Psalm 31:15 says God has perfect timing; he is never early or late, but always on TIME! God's perfect timing does two things: it grows our faith as we are forced to WAIT and trust him! What are you waiting on from God?

Grandiose men, again, are very blazing, very animated. Everything must be about them; They can care less about anyone, especially you. You must continue to feed their fantasies by sacrificing your dignity to do it. You see, these types of men live in a fantasy world and are the only stars in them! In this fantasy world they create, they're rich and grand but need you to constantly praise them, admire them, and stroke their egos. Like in the ancient days when kings and queensexisted, and the servants worshipped them on hands and knees. They feel entitled and will exploit other people to get whatever they feel is owed to them, which, my dear, would be you. Get this: they feel no shame, guilt, remorse, or anything as feelings go. You're just a vessel that gets them the bottom line, whatever they want, and they will intimate, bully, demeanor, and belittle you. Is that the kind of man you want to be with for the rest of your life, someone who only thinks about himself? If your answer is yes, then again, you're co-dependent.

My ex-husband would call me stupid and would talk to me as if I were his child; he never asked me to do something but instead ordered or demanded it of me. If I was at work, he would demand I leave my job and do whatever he needed to be done. What a butthole he was. He was never sorry or remorseful for anything he did. He would drink and smoke marijuana, which only made him act worse. He would choke me until I would pass out because I did not jump up and drop whatever I was doing to take care of what he wanted. These men are in love with themselves. They idolize their image.

My ex-husband had this idea he would be the king of trucks, so he pursued finding and buying used trucks for his business. He could buy two trucks with two drivers to drive them and just supervised them. He was the big BOSS in charge, letting everyone know it. He was living his DREAM! I didn't know at the time he only had a junior high education and could not read or write that well. And his family knew how. He was but did not happen to tell me at all. It was as if they had taken him off their hands because they were tired of helping to take care of his ungrateful, dysfunctional ass! He had no driver's license. It had expired. I took time to get his driver's and truck licenses, which were over a thousand dollars. He never said thank you anything, but why did you take so long to get them? I was getting fed up with him this time, so I left. He begged me to take him back; he was just stressed, he stated, and he was trying to do better and other lies to keep me in the relationship. Am I helping out any woman who has had these kinds of relationships, or worse, why?

Again, you are broken; you need some counseling anytime you allow a man to mistreat and abuse you for his selfish existence. Get out and get some counseling. I thought I loved my ex-husband, but I did not. It was my codependency kicking in and getting in the way of good judgement.

Everyone could see he was crazy except me. I had tunnel vision due to codependency. We, as co-dependent women, keep hooking up with narcissistic dysfunction and crazy-ass men for several reasons.

These guys' behaviors of abuse, neglect, and deceit are divorced from their consciousness that they are truly sick! They no longer feel pain or remorse nothing anymore. The Bible says be not deceived for God is not mocked for whatsoever a man soweth that shall he also reap Galatians 6:7. He got him after years of abuse, neglect, deceitfulness, and evilness. I divorced him. Yes, there is a God!

We hook up with these dysfunctional jokers due mostly to our codependency. We co-dependent women have lots of baggage from childhood and adulthood that reduces, in some cases, eliminates our self-esteem and self-worth. So, any little attention from these guys, dysfunctional and all, especially a good-looking one, comes as a pleasant surprise, not thinking he is narcissistic and wants to target me for self-gain. Not this cute, well-mannered, handsome guy! When you see horror shows, aren't the killers usually good-looking, or am I bugging you? We thank God for our fortune; this man came to talk to me! It's not God, but rather his opponent, Satan. He knows you're lonely, miserable, and damaged. After all, he had a hand in it, too! He was the cause of your mother drinking like mine, drugs like mine, and so forth and so on! That toxic guy will charm and lie his way into your life and make you more miserable than you were before you met his ass and broke! Somewomen who are too weak to fight this man and his treatment of them turn to drugs, alcohol, and abuse themselves, their kids, etc., as my mother did to my brother and me. Do you really want to repeat this cycle of abuse and neglect to your kids? Please don't do it; get some counseling and prayer!

At the beginning of this narcissistic relationship, they tend to treat us like princesses, which is extremely good. They make you feel special not because they value or care about you but to manipulate and control YOU! They gain control by playing up to our desires and needs so we feel special and highly valued. They tell us how cute and good-looking we are when they know that that may not be the truth. Since most of us are damaged, it catches you off guard, and for once, we enjoy the moment because that is all it is. They will create a close relationship and then move in to use tactics like shock, awe, and guilt to maintain control over again: YOU! The toxic, dysfunctional man comes later with control, drama, conflicts, pain, and heartache. You slowly start to feel neglected, have lower self-worth and lower self-esteem, and feelings of being trapped. Yes, you've been you've been fooled, baby; it was done skillfully by this predator.

I began to feel unappreciated and used as well as abused, and I was. You see, these narcissistic men use your childhood traumas as a tool to manipulate you into believing everything is your fault or you're responsible for fixing it. And that is whatever is wrong in the relationship; again, it's all your fault. My ex-husband acted like it was my fault he lost his license privileges. It was his!

I helped him get his license back and trucks to start his business. His reason for not having a job was he didn't want to work for the white man. WOW, because that was how I fed my family, and everyone else I knew did. I did not know back then when I was broken, that he had a plan in his mind to control me but did not feel comfortable enough to get that hook into me too soon. They go all out on a limb for you because they are practiced, liars and deceivers. They have been doing this to every woman they hook up with. And they get smarter as they continue these behaviors, learning how we women tick or operate. They study us and see what we will tolerate and not.

They create a plan in their minds for how they can take control of us and our lives. Yes, they aim to take over, control, and dominate you and your kids. Remember, as co-dependent women. We give up our power to these narcissistic men who thrive on this control and power.

Anyway, after several years of him not working, hustling, and driving for other people, I was able to purchase him one truck. Once he got that truck, he started working twelve to sixteen hours a day most days, but he kept his money. He did not buy groceries or pay any bills. He replied once when I asked him about his pay one Friday and why he doesn't help pay these bills. He replied this is your house, not mine, and those are your kids, not mine. You take care of them, not me! Yes, that was how much appreciation he showed me. A straight-up asshole! I was so damaged I had no clue.

As co-dependent women, we are very giving, sacrificial, and consumed with the needs and desires of others. We can't for the life of us figure out how to emotionally disconnect or avoid romantic relationships with toxic, dysfunctional, narcissistic men who are selfish, self-centered, controlling and harmful to us and our kids. We become martyrs (like Jesus) and sacrifice all, and I do mean all, our time, energy, money, and talent into these guys and the relationship, again because we're broken. To keep you in a toxic relationship, the narcissistic man will use a variety of tricks, tactics, and defenses to keep you insecure, which ensures their authoritative status while getting their needs met by you! Narcissistic men will give acceptance, respect, safety, and security at the beginning of a relationship, only to take it away. Most of the time, these relationships are often based on fear and vulnerability.

The second mental health narcissistic type of man is the vulnerable one. It is also called covert, closet, or introvert. An Introvert is a person who is not sociable; they feel better focusing on themselves and being with a few people, whereas the extrovert loves crowds of people. These guys shay away from any attention yet are self-absorbed, entitled, exploitative, unempathetic, manipulative, and aggressive. But get this: they fear criticism; they can't stand to hear you murmur one single criticism about them. You left the toilet seat up again; why do you dress like a mat, so torn and so on? They are insecure, unhappy, and have more stress than you do, who have a job every day while they stay at home doing nothing! They're constantly anxious, depressed, hypersensitive, and shameful. The narcissistic, vulnerable man can be negative all the time, bitter, and. angry. No lie, but my ex-husband woke up mad every single day and never said good morning. When I would say it, his reply was what's so good about it! Red Flag, Red Flag! And when he drank, which was all the time, he became mentally and physically abusive. These men withdraw from others and are hostile and always blame others for their misfortunes, bad life, no job, you name it. As their woman, we feel sorry for them and want to rescue them from their misery. We try to give them anything they want but end up self-sacrificing our feelings of responsibility for them.

These vulnerable men shy away from attention and lack autonomy. They have this syndrome called the imposter syndrome, in which they have a weak sense of self-identity which makes it even harder for them to navigate their environment. They feel depressed and peséimistic and feel like they got the short end of the stick in life. They are also hypersensitive to any type of criticism and will even go as far as to throw tantrums like a child. They look for women with a positive outlook on life and see the best in them. This works for them since these men can't be empathetic with anyone, not less you. These men are bitter and negative all the time.

What a bummer, uh? They often lack positive relationships. Often, they are loners, always by themselves. However, they will dominate, threaten and hurt you. Their style is avoidance, anxiety, withdrawal from you, and having the nerve to be mad, hostile, blaming YOU for their life and misfortunes, and resentful towards you! I told you these men are crazy! But what do we do? We feel sorry for them and try to rescue (remember, co-dependent s want to sacrifice themselves for our men) them from misery but end up self-scarifying and feeling responsible for them. That again further destroys our self-esteem and self-worth. Leave that bugger alone and keep it moving!

The third jackass, my bag narcissistic man, is the communal narcissistic type of man. These jokers are sorry again, but these guys lack empathy and value warmth. Uh, how does that go? They want to be seen by others as trustworthy, friendly, kind, and supportive to gain your trust. Red flag! He is a sneaky individual so friendly you don't even realize it until he rapes, murders, or harms you. He is sort of like the child pedophile who is friendly and offers candy to the victims before he molests them. In reality, he is antisocial aggressive, and has no regard for other people like most serial killers. These narcissistic men say stuff like they want to save mankind from some sort of disaster and seek recognition and validation for anything they do, sort of like the grandiose; they just want to be praised and recognized! They display outward giving, caring, and helpfulness; that's how they talk to you. Also, if you drop a package or food item in a store, they will rush to help you pick it up, that sort of creep. These guys have high self-esteem, feel entitled, and are also very dangerous types of men. Let that joker go on his merry way and wait for God to send you a REAL man. Get help and counseling before you make a big decision by getting involved with these narcissistic men. Again, they will make your life a living hell. That's how I lived the many long and terrible years I was with my narcissistic ex-husband.

The last and fourth narcissistic man is the malignant narcissistic one who is extremely mean and EVIL! Stay away from his sick and crazy ass, for real. Run for the hills and block his number on your phone. They are the real serial killers, murderers, burglars, you name it, anything terrible is this individual. They are cruel, aggressive, cold, and not a good person to be in a relationship with.

They can be paranoid (who would figure that one out), immortal, and sadistic, like Charles Manson, the convicted cult leader who organized nine murders in California in August of 1969. He believed he was some sort of messiah and would save the world from destruction. He was a sick, malignant, selfish man who spent forty years in prison and died there. That is all evil will do for you: use and discard you. That is what narcissistic men do, too, so be very careful when you meet people. Now that you have an idea how these jokers operate, you can leave them alone and wait on a good man, not a psychotic one.

Another very sick individual and narcissistic was Bernie Madoff, who created a Ponzi scheme 'in 2008 that wiped out millions of dollars from unsuspected people he knew and did business with. This scheme also ruined charities that he funded, all in the name of greed, evil, and malignant narcissism. This Ponzi scheme was said to be the largest in Wall Street history. Sad to say, but Madoff was convicted and died in jail as well. Something is truly wrong when someone intentionally wants to harm and hurt people; they have to be sick, psychotic, and narcissistic. These men take pleasure, PLEASURE in creating chaos and taking people down; it's like a game to them. These malignant narcissistic guys are closely related to psychopathy and antisocial personality disorder.

I know you're lonely and broken, but if you become involved with this man, you will regret it for the rest of your life. This relationship will drain you, not meet your needs, and constantly criticize you. If you ask for something, they will meet your request with anger, aggression, outrage, and the cold shoulder treatment! Isn't that a bitch! They will view you as an object with one purpose: serving him and his needs. He will frequently intimidate you, bully you, belittle you, and will not ever recognize your wants or needs. They don't really want a partner. Instead, they are looking for someone who will obey and admire them like the Manson followers. He ordered them to kill nine people, and they did as he stood there and watched, what a sick and psychotic person he was. You know the story: his mother was a prostitute, and he grew up in foster homes and jails, the same old story as some of us broken people. It's a game to them you are, and they play only to get power over YOU! They are self-obsessed who control others for their gain. Did you get the part where they use YOU for their gain?

Narcissistic men are toxic as well as dysfunctional; they are damaged, and if challenged, they will fight you, throw temper tantrums, make excuses, deny, blame, and they are hypersensitive. www.psychologytoday.com. He may even, if criticized, take flight and bolt out the door to avoid confrontation with you, or sulk around the house, become bitter and resentful, all designed to control. If you act like you're getting tired of their drama all the time, they will become upset at any sign of independence and self-affirmation and have unpredictable swings, all designed to keep and maintain control over YOU! By keeping you down and making you feel inferior, this boosts their fragile ego, thus making them more assured about themselves. You see, they project false, idealized images of themselves to the world to hide their insecurities because they want to impress you. They make themselves look good externally to tell us I'm a big deal and worthy of everyone's love, devotion, admiration, and acceptance; that's what my ex-husband did when he had those trucks; his chest and head got big! His family was impressed and told him so. He ate the shit up, while I was the one that sacrificed everything financially, did without me and my kids to help him get those two trucks.

And to keep you in this dysfunctional relationship, they use several tactics to keep control of you. I will only mention one, for there are others, but we'll use the gas lighting technique for time's sake. This one is a very severe abusive tactic to keep you in their control. Narcissistic men use it to manipulate, control, and, yes, even brainwash you daily.

The reason they use it is because it's EFFECTIVE! This technique helps these men to get, gain, maintain, and control their minds and, thus, their behavior. After all, they gain your life and your money, and it is only a sport to them. Remember, these men are practiced actors and manipulators; they do this for a living.

They target co-dependent women because these types of women are easy and guaranteed success due to their dysfunctional environment as a child. The traumas, abuse, rape, poor home life, and low self-esteem. A woman who is not damaged can see through their tricks, so they avoid them and choose YOU!

Gas lighting is extremely destructive and starts slow and subtle, so slow you don't even see it. This form of abuse can cause you to lose your sense of your self-identity. They use gas lighting to weaken and stabilize you again to gain control over YOU! They'll use tactics to trick you, like positive and negative emotions. Good today with you; tomorrow, they are mad at you with back-and-forth emotions. These are designed too to try and control YOU!

These narcissistic, malignant men will always resort to escalation of emotions by doubling down on their tactics of false accusations, coercions, or whatever they can use to ultimately oppress you and get this; they even view this or any relationship as competitive instead of collaborative! Told you they were a very sick individual and dangerous, too. These men will perform emotionally charged tantrums, too, as they will do so when something upsets or disappoints them. In my case, if I had not agreed to help my ex-husband get those trucks, he would have become violent. So, what do us co-dependent, dysfunctional women do? We work harder to please them so they will not go OFF again.

There are several gas lighting techniques used by malignant narcissistic men, namely lying, exaggerating, and disputing, that escalate. With lying and exaggerating, he will play mind games with you by saying something mean, ugly, or downright nasty about you and your shortcomings something like 'you plain looking or did you gain more weight? Or how come you're so unattractive," which causes you to become defensive, anxious, and upset. These narcissistic men will repeat daily these gas lighting tactics to gain control over you, making you constantly nervous and offensive. He does this again to dominate your relationship and keep him in control of you. If you are broken, remember this because for a person who is not broken, this stuff will not work, and he knows that, again, that's why he chose YOU!

Another gaslight tactic is to dispute and escalate, another ignorant mind game. They will challenge you, so when they call you out on theirs, not your lies, they will produce evidence to prove whatever they're saying you are, such as you can't even cook food without it burning and producing a burned food item, something like that. You may be thinking I didn't do that and say that, but he may say no one else is here in the house but the two of us, so who did it? He's trying to mess with your mind, and again, if you're broken and co-dependent, it works. He then will blame you, try to put doubt in your mind, and add more false claims about what you didn't do. You then get so confused that it becomes hard to tell who is right or wrong.

Again, only damages women because a woman who is not damaged will let these jokers go and keep it moving. A woman who has it together will not tolerate these types of manipulative mind games. But when you're broken, you accept anything from a narcissistic man due to your low self-worth and low self-esteem. You feel like you can't do any better. Look how I look, overweight, fat, ugly, plain, depressed; who would want to be with me, you think to yourself. You are unable to be co-dependent, incapable of choosing a giving and unconditionally loving man. You sabotage a good man in a good relationship unconsciously because you're motivated to find someone familiar to your dysfunctional self-reminiscent of your powerless and traumatic childhood. Your fear of being alone and your compulsion to fix at any cost is another reason why you stay in these dysfunctional relationships. You see your comfort in the role of a martyr, which is endlessly loving and devoted, an extension of the need to be loved, respected, and cared for when you were a child.

These narcissistic, malignant men will concentrate on making YOU feel inferior through false accusations like infidelity-producing men's clothing, constant criticism, and or psychological intimidation. He plans to wear you down by being offensive all the time. You will start to feel like you're doubting yourself and get discouraged, fearful, and debilitated. At some point, you start to doubt reality about who you are and if you're perceiving things right. In gas lighting, the man will treat you at times really nice, kind, and sweet, then a couple of hours later, he will become ignorant and nasty again like Dr. Jackel and Mr. Hyde! Once these men get you into a relationship with them, they feel they can cheat and physically and mentally abuse you, which they deny doing anything wrong. For some victims who may have fragile minds like cult followers, it can cause suicide or nervous breakdown. Members of the Manson and David Koresh cult did just that.

This tactic is to give you false hope in this relationship. This is a manipulative ploy to make you think he is not so bad and can get better. The nice and kind act is part of his plan to manipulate and control YOU! You become off-guard, which allows this man to begin his next step of mental abuse, which reinforces your codependency. These narcissistic men's goal again is to have total control of our minds, where we are dominated and controlled without any consequences.

That is what Manson did to his cult followers; he took control of their minds, and he had them murder innocent people, nine in all. And the whole goal of this gaslight tactic is to make you doubt yourself and control your mind as Manson and other cult leaders did. Remember cult leader David Koresh in Waco, Texas, in April 1993. He had his cult members armed themselves with guns and had a shootout with police and FBI, which ended in a fire destroying the whole building, and most members died, including the leader David. Karma is a mother, isn't she? This David cult leader, like Manson, told his followers he was some sort of Messiah, using this to sleep with female members, including girls 12 years of age, and called them his wives. He brainwashed these men and women and children followers, ending in their deaths during the shootout with law enforcement.

He was crazy, a narcissistic, malignant man who had trauma in his childhood, too. It still boils down to a CHOICE! Yours! God gives us free will. You can choose eternal life with God or eternal HELL with Satan. The choice is yours! Some argue that there is no God! I beg to differ; the earth and everything in it did not magically appear out of the blue one day. It doesn't work like that, be for real. 'The only thing the Devil will bring is death and destruction!

Sorry to say, but there is no cure for these individuals, only therapy and counseling. However, few men want to get the help because they don't believe in their minds that they have a problem.'

Satan has their mind and has them thinking that they are all that matters, not no one else. In a healthy and normal relationship, both people can be intimate and get this. Neither has ALL the POWER! It is shared!

Chapter 3 How to Avoid the Pitfalls of a Codependency Relationship

Codependency sometimes is hard to overcome, especially if it is a lifelong struggle like I had. It can become a learned behavior from past traumas, usually in your childhood. In codependency, your support is so extreme that it becomes unhealthy for you. You try to control and save the actions and moods of other people. You may have had boundaries but no longer have them. And you need boundaries so people know how far to go or push you. Healthy people have them, but if you're broken, you do not. You turn into a martyr and always try to fix stuff. You may not intentionally do this, but over time, that person comes to depend on your help and does less for themselves. You feel a sense of purpose, even fulfilment, from sacrificing all your needs for someone else. In which they will never feel appreciative, so you do more and more for them. You repeat these unhealthy patterns of controlling and sacrificing over and over until you can't stop. This is a learned behavior again from your childhood traumas, neglect, and abuse like me! You see, the real reason you do it is you rely on other people to validate who you are instead of yourself!

We keep saying codependency is usually rooted or caused by childhood trauma, abuse, and neglect, and it's true. As a child, you seek acceptance, approval, and love from your caregivers, parents, grandparents, siblings, neighbors, and friends. They validate your gender, either a girl or a boy. If you're a girl, you wear pastel colors of pink, yellow, white, etc. And as a boy, you usually dress in blues, greens, and tans. Your family tells you how cute you are, as a girl, how pretty you are, and dress you in ruffled dresses with lace socks because that is how I dress my girls. You put barrettes and ribbons in their hair with pretty braids or curls. You know you're a pretty little girl because everyone you know and love says the same thing. That is validation for you, and as you grow into a young woman, your family continues to validate your beauty, intelligence, and acceptance and approval of you. This makes you grow into a healthy, competent woman.

But what happens when you get the opposite of everything that makes you a competent, healthy woman? What happens when, instead of pretty dresses, people tell you how bad you look, and you have no pretty dresses, shoes, or socks? What happens when you are belittled, berated, neglected, physically and mentally abused, and raped like I was, what happens to you then? Well, you become co-dependent, damaged, with low self-esteem, low self-worth, and broken, lacking confidence like me. Sometimes, people turn into a serial killer who hates people and blame them for their anger, pain, misery, and outcome in their life of crime. And the pain, it seems, never goes away unless you get tired and do something about it, like suicide or overdose of pills like people you hear about every day. You need help from a licensed therapist, counselor, and GOD!

Therapy is like a nurse; it helps nurse your mind and body back to a healthy state with caring nonjudgmental care. They start in your childhood to help you understand how you got broken at first. Mine was from an alcoholic mother and an absent father. My mother was critical of everything that I did; I could do nothing right. I was a child starting at five; how could l? She would call me stupid, slow, or dumb all in one sentence. As I began to grow up, it got worse, daily belittling and degrading. You didn't do this right or that right. Why are you so stupid? This made me feel stupid since she kept saying I was. But I always had good grades, an A student in school, which I loved, so I found my salvation in reading. I became a nerd. I only wanted to read romantic novels of love, admiration, and beauty (because I had picky nappy hair and coke-bottled horn-rimmed glasses) and was never told I was pretty or loved. My mother made me feel worthless, and on top of all of Viat, I had to care for my baby brother because my mother was drunk and asleep most of the daytime. I had to dress and feed the both of us until he got older and could do it himself.

So, to overcome the pitfalls of codependency, number one is you got it, get HELP! There is nothing, and I do mean nothing wrong with getting help. I waited until my fifties to get some help after a nasty divorce. If my family had not pushed me to do it, I would still be stuck on stupid and in a dysfunctional, abusive relationship with a narcissistic man! I was in big-time denial (five steps of grieving). Therapists go back to the beginning of your life, your childhood, and rebuild that foundation that makes you confident, building your self-esteem and self-worth usually, dysfunctional people come from toxic and dysfunctional environments like I did. You come from poor and humble beginnings, drugs or alcohol or other substances abuse. Often you may have suffered in silence guilt and shame from rape as a child like me. No one knows, but rape victims know how they can change your life. Some rape victims become promiscuous or, like me, frigid. Tyler Perry made a movie called ADDICTED, about a woman who was raped as a child on a playground and became an adult married woman who became promiscuous outside her marriage. She had two other lovers; she was a sex addict due to rape at a young age; that was how she handled her trauma. I did the opposite. I became frigid and, for most of my adult life, had trouble with intimacy, so much so every one of my ex-husbands cheated on me. I know it was not all their fault now since I've been healed of my brokenness. But when, I knew something was wrong with me; I just could not figure out what!

Next, you must identify patterns in your life that make you want to be co-dependent health. Stay in your lane, and remember you can ONLY CONTROL your actions, not anyone else! When we take care of other people and their needs, we then sacrifice our needs, which causes a chain reaction. We get sick, irritable, resentful, impatient, and disconnected from ourselves, and YOU become depressed, lonely, and anxious. Establish boundaries in your relationships. Resist the urge to fix, control, and save other people.

Codependency behavior is a way to control or direct someone's behavior or mood from doing that. Your partner picks up a learned co-dependent behavior from you because you keep controlling them, so they do less for themselves. Again, you fall into this pattern of feeling good and purposeful from sacrificing your needs and wants for your partner! STOP! You're doing it again, codependency! This is a pattern: learn to stop doing this. Patterns you learn in childhood you can learn to repeat in adulthood, but you must identify them and put a stop to them! It's a lifelong struggle to break, but you can do this, especially if you've been in therapy. But first, get some professional help.

Do you always gravitate to helpless people like those in your family, friends, or work? Self-sacrificing often makes you feel closer to your mate. I can't figure out why because God knows they don't appreciate what you do for them. Trust me; I know because I sacrificed my money, friends, and family for my ex-husband that left me feeling empty and drained!

Identifying these patterns is the key to overcoming them. Talk to yourself; sometimes you have to do that.

Tell yourself I'm doing it again; my codependency is kicking in, so stop it now, girl! Not all unhealthy page relationships are co-dependent, but all co-dependent relationships are UNHEALTHY!

Learn what healthy relationships look like. A healthy love relationship involves comfort, support, contentment, and, of course, LOVE! An unhealthy relationship consists of pain, despair, dysfunction, arguing, fusing, and fighting. Does this sound like your relationship? Get out and get some help! A healthy relationship offers so much more than that foolishness. The only explanation for you going through that type of treatment again is you're broken; please get some professional help. Only you and you must fix the broken pieces of yourself to heal that inner child because that is the one that needs healing!

A healthy relationship will enrich and add to your life; it does not take away. Instead of anger, confusion, and misery (devil), it will comfort, nourish, and love you, leaving you with peace (God). Signs of a healthy relationship include trust; each of you trusts the other. Now, I'm talking about monogamous relationships, not the ones with three or four or more partners, because God did not create those types of relationships; the devil did. And again, his goal is to take as many souls as possible to HELL with him as he can by convincing you it is okay. It is not okay, and God is not pleased; that's why those relationships don't work. Then, in a monogamous relationship, both partners feel secure, secure, I said, in their self-worth. Like I now have, I know who I am and whose I belong to, my Savior. In a healthy relationship, NO ONE has all the power; it is shared, and you compromise when needed. In a healthy relationship, your partner cares and loves you, and get this: they don't want anything from you but your love and devotion! You feel safe to share all your true feelings with your partner, and you tell your partner all your emotional needs, not like codependency. In codependency, you try to control and fix your partner; that's how you know it's codependency.

Also, in a healthy relationship, you can voice your opinions even if your partner has a different one. You can say NO, especially if it differs from theirs. You can set boundaries in a healthy relationship and tell them to your partner because they also have boundaries. Remember, a boundary is a limit you set around things you're uncomfortable with, such as physical touching. I am not comfortable being touched by people I don't know or the way you speak to me (due mostly to my abuse). Boundaries may be hard for some, especially if you're going through therapy for codependency issues. For me, I was so used to taking care of and making my ex comfortable that I never considered my limits, and I had no boundaries. However, I do now I've learned to trust myself. And you can learn, too, but only with counseling. Remember, some of your behaviors are learned, and you've been carrying them all your life, like me. It will take time, but you are a phenomenal woman like me; you got this! Remember also you're never alone; God is always with you. You may not be able to see or track him, but trust me, you can TRUST him; I am a witness!

Why are boundaries so important? Well, doesn't every house have walls and a front door? It's there to keep the occupants SAFE and intruders out. That is what boundaries do; they tell people to stop at your front door and not go any farther. So, honor your boundaries; they're there for a good reason. Listen to what people say empathetically, but stop trying to FIX their problems; let them figure it out for themselves. Aren't they adults and GROWN? Practice saying NO, NO, and NO. It will start to feel good and powerful when you do it often enough. People tend to take your kindness, goodness, or whatever for a weakness; it's not. Your partner should want and value you for who you are (love), not what you have (money) and not what you can do for HIM! That's not a healthy relationship; that is some codependency stuff!

No, you can't borrow my money, car, or anything else to get your own shit! Once you start setting boundaries, the people you have been bending over and taking care of will come to a wide awakening. I can't use her anymore! You mean you're not going to take care of me first? When you fly on an airplane, the stewards explain what to do if the plane starts malfunctioning (God forbid), but she says if the cabin pressure drops, you will automatically see an oxygen mask fall in front of you. What do you do next, ladies? First, apply to YOUR face, then reach up and put on someone else's face, usually a child. You must take care of yourself FIRST. Stop waiting for someone else to care for you because it may not happen. This will only make you frustrated, anxious, angry, and all sorts of feelings, putting you back in the codependency cycle! Don't get free only to put yourself back in slavery via emotional chains again!

Codependency is a tough cookie to crumble (old saying), but not impossible. Remember you can control only YOUR own thoughts, behaviors, and actions. Trying to control someone else's behaviors or actions usually doesn't work out, plus you become frustrated! Have you ever wanted something for someone so bad, but they didn't want it for themselves? Yes, well, I have; my daughter has a beautiful voice, but she hides hers like the servant with a talent. I want to push her to get out there and use her talent, but she will not. I realised a long time ago I can't do it for her. She has to want to do it for herself! Giving up control over other people involves accepting uncertainties. Yes, life is full of them.

No one knows the future, especially if you're afraid of being alone. Losing someone due to codependency issues like control is hard, or not being able to have boundaries, so you stay quiet and not make your own needs known. If you're in a healthy relationship with a healthy partner, it is more than likely to last and weather any storms that may occur. I'm not saying not to help or support someone you love, but you can offer healthy support. You can help anyone you want, but don't sacrifice your needs or wants. That's called codependency! Don't confuse PITY with LOVE.

How to Stop Being Co-dependent, Recognizing and Moving Past Codependency, Fuller, Kristine 12-3-2018. Figure out where your expectations for a relationship are coming from. A place deep down inside of you from past disappointments and resentments because this can affect how you interact in your present relationship. It's called baggage; leave it at your front door. Please do not bring it into your new relationship; it will only confuse you and make you lapse into codependency AGAIN!

Healthy support involves talking about someone's problems with them to HELP them come up with a solution. After all, it is their problem, not YOURS! You can offer a good ear for your loved one's worries, concerns, or problems. Sometimes, people just want someone to talk to, not solve their problems for them. Discuss with your loved one and suggest possible solutions rather than for them. Again, I don't care what you suggest; some people will not accept your suggestion. Some people are co-dependent, some people want to hear themselves talk, and some again just want to VENT! Offer advice when asked, not before; they may not be ready to hear it anyway. Let them make their own decision while offering them acceptance and compassion.

Learn to love and value yourself, the real YOU! Doesn't our God wonderfully and beautifully create you? I know I am just sorry because of my brokenness (devil). I didn't know it at that time in my life. But I do now! Practice valuing yourself because codependency and low   self-esteem always hang out together. You will not see one without the other! Increase your self-worth, confidence, happiness, and self-esteem. Let yourself change instead of taking all your energy to change others! Did you get that you made the change? Channel all your energy into YOU? Improve YOU, for once, instead of someone else. If you do this, you will be able to express your wants and needs more easily and help yourself to set your boundaries, too. These are keys to overcoming codependency.

Always protect yourself; if the relationship starts to go south (physical and mental abuse, neglect, demeaning, and belittling you), then get out! Vulnerability and intimacy are forms of connection that must be earned. You build them steadily over time, not tossed around recklessly. And freely telling someone you just met all your info is not cool; it is a sign that you have no boundaries. Most abusive relationships start like magic: nothing and no one ever treated you so well! Then, slowly, the toxic dysfunction comes out. He will start cursing and calling you names rather than physical abuse. That's how it happened to me. My ex-husband bought me candy and flowers at first, picnics in the park and such, you name it, then the arguing over petty stuff got worse shortly after. Because I was broken, I accepted this as love; it was not. It was codependency masquerading as LOVE! When you love someone, you're not supposed to hear insults, belittles, name-calling, or anything like that because it's not healthy. It's dysfunctional.

My husband and I have been together for seven years and have never not once had a fight or argument. We COMMUNICATE; that's what people do who love each other! Speak up for yourself; you have OPTIONS! YOU deserve love and respect as a human being with all your flaws and imperfections. Again, there was only one man without sin; his name was and still is CHRIST! Soothing, comfort, validation, and empathy are critical to any relationship! It is DANGEROUS to make someone YOUR EVERYTHING! If you do it again, you are co-dependent and broken.

Value yourself by spending time with the people who treat you with love, kindness, and respect! Now don't go spend time with your toxic and dysfunctional family members who will piss you off, frustrate and make you mad, causing you to slip back into your codependency habit of saving them and sacrificing YOU! Stay away from them, honey. It isn't worth making YOU feel blue! Instead, hang out with girlfriends you enjoy being with, go out for drinks, dinner, dancing, or whatever makes you feel good about yourself. Go shopping with some co-workers or girlfriends, buy some shoes (my favorite pastime), take dancing classes (I did line classes), gather some friends and go to concerts, travelling (I do that with my husband and cousin; we love to cruise) and many more options you see life is full of them.

Spend YOUR time with positive people, not people full of gloom and doom folks who will drain you, and you know who they are. I can picture it now. I had an older aunt, and anytime, I do mean anytime you asked her how she felt, she would launch into how horrible she felt, how bad her day was going, and on and on for hours, no kidding! It got to a point where I had my issues, so I stopped asking her how she felt; instead, I would just say "HI" and keep moving. Spend time with people who value YOU as a person and not for what you have or can do for them either. Surround yourself with people who are positive, offer acceptance, and support YOU! Don't wait for people to appreciate you and compliment you; instead, appreciate and compliment yourself. I do every day. My coworkers call me a "Diva," and I'm the definition of one! I TAKE SO GOOD CARE OF ME now! I've learned since counseling that I'm IMPORTANT TO ME!

Do things that please YOU. I sew quilts, find and search puzzles, play solitaire on my phone, and shop on my phone; my favorite site is Fashion Nova! Pursue your passions only. YOU hold the key to your happiness. Follow your inspirations. Is there something you dream about? If you dream it, you can do it! Is there a dream you dream about doing? My dream was to write a book and look, I DID IT! I also wanted to marry Prince Charming, my knight in shining armor. I did that, too! The front of my first book was of me on my wedding day; it was so beautiful. Thank You, Lord, for fulfilling my dreams and sending my Prince to me! We travel, go to the park, and take long walks together. Life is GOOD, and so is GOD! All the time, and all the time, God is GOOD! The skies are the limit (old but true saying)! Set aside some time every day God gives you (it's called a present) and do things that give you pleasure. Never forget to thank God for all he does in your life! I love ice cream, Blue Bell butter pecan, and Dairy Queen's blizzards (I only limit it to occasionally;

you know I'm dairy intolerant). If you don't pursue your interest, it will only lead to discontent and regret.

Take care of your health; that is the most important thing to do if you want to be around for a long time. I do. See your doctor regularly, especially if you have health issues like mine. Eat healthy and limit your unhealthy foods like fast and fried foods (they are no good; they just clog your arteries up). Get plenty of sleep, 8 hours at least, and exercise every day for 30 minutes or more. If you don't like exercising, walk outside, smell the flowers, cut grass, hear birds chirping, and thank God you were alive to see a day you have never seen before. Lose weight if you are overweight; get my book for tips on slimming down like I did. Come on, you got this. You can do anything you set your mind to; I did, and you can too!

If you're stuck in the codependency mode, admit it to yourself and get some professional help. Not your mother, father, sister, brother, or the minister, school nurse, unless they are licensed therapists! Even though you can discuss with those individuals, more than likely, it will not help YOU! Prioritize YOU; relationships are supposed to complement your life, NOT be YOUR LIFE! And if you're in an abusive relationship, have enough sense to get out and get some professional HELP! Love yourself enough to speak up and ask for what you need and want. Don't expect other people, especially your partner, to read your mind (not a fortune teller); it will only make you resentful, and that leads to pain, which turns quickly into PITY, 10 Ways to Love Yourself and Heal from Codependency Lanier, Darlene. Instead of looking for approval from other people, value YOURSELF! Most of the time, codependency looks to others for validation and approval.

However, when we do that, we give our POWER away and allow others to determine our value and worth instead of letting us decide for ourselves. We should learn to build our self-esteem and LOVE and value ourselves. We do that by taking note of our strengths and forgiving ourselves for all the many mistakes we've made. And most importantly, remember LOVE doesn't have to be earned. We are all inherently worthy and IMPORTANT! 7 WAYS TO Avoid Codependency in Your Relationship, Martin, Sharon 2-8-2019.

Life is tough and can and will get rough sometimes, but for the most part, it's supposed to also be enjoyed! Instead of being a martyr, get professional help if you need it! Stop feeling sorry for yourself, get off the couch, and LIVE! Most co-dependent individuals HATE ask for help; they feel it makes them look weak! It does not; it makes you look SMART! Go out and do what my cousin told me to do (now she says to slow down; I'm having too much fun now). Enjoy life and yourself, laugh, relax; take bubble baths with scented beads and a candle all around the tub with music low by yourself, or live me with somebody (1 get my hubby)! Do activities that rejuvenate you. Do stuff you never did before, like hiking, zip lining, you name it! Pleasure helps YOU restore your energy and sense of well-being, so much so that you will be nourished to your soul. It's like food; once you enjoy something, you feel good after eating it. Am I right or what? The bottom line is you are important, and find someone who feels the same way about you that you do! Good men are out there; what are you waiting on? They will not come knocking on your door. You'll have to go out and find one for yourself!' Dress fiercely, look good, smell good, and wear heels; what normal heterosexual men can resist that?

Chapter 4 Putting Everything Together to Reinvent ME, After Codependency!

To be honest with you, being co-dependent like I was and now living a life with no codependency is exhilarating, exciting, and exceptional. Not only did I free myself of the codependency demons, but at last, I found my true passion and purpose in my life. Praise God! The Devil had me in a fog, and therapy for codependency brought me out of the fog into the sunshine, where there were no clouds or fog. I can see clearly now; The Rain Has Gone is an old but true song by Johnnie Nash. I now stay away from people, places, and situations that can and will if I'm not careful to slip back into that negativity and codependency. So, you may be wondering how that is done. Again, therapy is the true savior sort of speak, along with support very, very important from family and friends. Spirituality for me (was God) and time, patience with myself, and love for myself most of all. Once you reinvent yourself, you can take yourself to limitless happiness in your wildest dreams because that is what I'm doing now. Who knew I would one day be an author or married again, this time to my soul mate? Who knew, God did! He was waiting for me to finally get myself together with therapy, family support, and God's love for me! Yes, reinvention is possible, and so is a life without co-dependency!

You've got to rebalance speak your whole being How to Conquer codependency Sharon Martin 10-20-2020. You, first of all, above everything else, LOVE GOD and YOURSELF! You've got to believe in yourself and your ability to heal from codependency. And you have to make it a habit! You need resilience or the ability to adapt in the face of adversity; the better you know yourself, the better your chance for success. You need to focus on YOU for once in your life! Recovery is an ACTION word and is a PARAMOUNT part of this process. What you need and want for YOU, and not worry about anyone else's needs or wants at this time in your reinvention of YOU! Your self-esteem will give you more confidence without having to use drugs or alcohol to negotiate new situations or people. You've got to make yourself understand your needs and wants are just as important as anyone else. If you don't take care of your needs, you'll become resentful, depleted, and unfulfilled again, like in codependency. Is that what you want to happen AGAIN? Healing involves sometimes not knowing what you need but instead ASK for something once again in your life! We are no longer martyrs or victims anymore. We must learn to stand up for ourselves, our needs, and our wants. We've got to set boundaries and stop people from crossing them as if they're not there so we can protect ourselves from any more mistreatment, abuse, or neglect.

Learn to find your VOICE! Say NO when you mean NO! Losing someone, a friend, family, or man is okay, especially if they cannot respect your boundaries. Boundaries are a sign of a healthy person that would now be YOU! Co-dependent s HAVE no boundaries, and that is one of the major reasons that they draw toxic narcissistic type men. We want healthy relationships where we give and receive for once! And while you're at it, take EXPECTATIONS out of your relationships. These are relationship killers! These expectations can be a source of pressure to make someone feel the pressure of meeting your wants and needs specifically! Remember, relationships are supposed to COMPLEMENT you, not DEFINE.

We've got to explore who we really are, what we like or dislike, what's important in our lives, and set goals for ourselves. Do you want to go back to school or learn a new trade? It's your life, and you have my permission (not that you ever needed it) to do anything you want to NOW! We need to pamper ourselves and treat us with kindness, love, and acceptance. Yes, we have gotten a bad turn in life, but there is an old saying: when life gives you lemons, turn around and make some sweet old lemonade, not hater aid! Stop being the VICTIM! As a co-dependent, I was hard on myself. I used to think, why am 1 letting this man do such terrible and abusive things to me? I was self-critical and unforgiving of myself. I'm not stupid; I have a bachelor's degree in nursing, yet I could not figure out how to not be mistreated! I knew the answer: I was just broken, and he took advantage of that. I had to let all that hurt, pain, and anger go. It was unhealthy, unhelpful, unkind, and unwarranted to me. I need self-compassion, which increases my resilience and motivation and decreases stress. I now know I'm an incredible, intelligent, beautiful, smart black woman, and NO ONE will ever be able to take that away from me!

You've got to learn that you are valued and have worth; you had it all along. You just didn't know it at the time you were broken (co-dependent)! You now have to live from that place of self-autonomy and love for everything you represent WITHOUT needing anyone anymore to validate you, How to Reclaim Your Awesomeness from The Grips of Codependency Matt Landsiedel 8-5-2019

Here are a few helpful suggestions if you don't know how to jump-start this new you! First again, I'll keep saying it: LOVE yourself and God (or your spiritual entity). Take time for yourself and spend time with you. Get reacquainted with YOU! Spend more time at church, read the Bible, and listen to sermons. I go online to YouTube and listen and watch various ministers and church services: God is good all the time, and all the time, God is good! Go shopping, walk, and listen to some music. I love oldies and soul music. Nothing makes me happier than Aretha, Temptations,

Four Tops, you get the draft. I go to the park, put Pandora on my phone, sit under a tree, and enjoy LIFE! And thank God for my reinvention and life free of codependency. I take long bubble baths with my soul music, playing some Otis or Bobby Bland blues! I light candles and stay in the tub for hours, soaking and reheating the water with hot water. When I get out, my skin is wrinkled and pink. I feel renewed and rejuvenated; it is an awesome feeling!

I started sewing and now make quilts for my grandkids, daughters, and friends. I made a beautiful white one for my best friend. Who knew not me that I could sew, but I was raised in a household of alcohols who sewed. So, I saw them sew when I was a kid and picked it up recently; who knew? God did; he's helping me find some more of my talents. What he has done for others, he'll do the same for you! Try a new hobby or craft; my next hobby will be crocheting or knitting. I have a church member who crochets beautifully; she made me a scarf, which has inspired me; when I was a kid, my grandmother used to crochet. I still have a sweater she crocheted for me. Think of something in your past you may want to pursue, like knitting, pottery classes, or sewing classes, to reconnect with friends, coworkers, and family. I started a girl's night out at work one night a month on the last Friday of the month. And five of my coworkers go out to eat at different ones, a movie, or out for drinks. We had so much fun, and I started it four or five years ago. I was new to the area and did not know where to eat, so I started asking coworkers to go with me to eat, and we have been doing it since. We've turned into a support group for one another. We cheer for victories, cry for disappointments, and give out advise to each other. Have some fun and enjoy your newfound self. I did that excellently. My cousin told me your fun pass has expired. You've taken fun to a whole another level, and I have! You only get one life and one time to enjoy it. I got to make up for lost time in all those years of codependency, you know! Pleasure helps to restore your energy and sense of well-being, which in turn nourishes your soul and enhances your productivity and work quality, 10 Ways to Love Yourself and Heal from Codependency by Darlene Lancer.

The biggest help to me was therapy. That was the best thing I could have done for myself. For co-dependent people, that is hard to do! You are so used to people needing you instead of the opposed, and you need some help! If you feel lonely, which you may sometimes feel anxious, overwhelmed, or depressed, reach out to someone you love and trust. I had great family and friends. All I had to do was call them; they remember, without balance, your pain or anger can and will turn into self-pity and can pull you back into co-dependency. Don't let it do that to you, please!

Chapter 5
Women Walking by Faith are Walking in the Spirit

The question is asked... How do I take a broken life, lost loves, and unfulfilled dreams and allow God to use them for both His glory and my walk on the pathway to growth in my life? First, must be willing to trust god with my broken life and all of its broken iecës in doin' so I recognize God is bigger and greater than my fears, weaknesses, and energies come in I must learn to wait patiently, knowing that God will meet all of my needs God knows the number of hairs on our head, surly God knows and cares for those walking by faith. Luke 1 2:7... says, "But the very hairs of your head are all numbered. Do not fear, therefore; you are of more value than many sparrows." God knows every hair on our heads, so how could He not know what is best for those walking by faith?

The phrase 'walk in the Spirit' means to walk continuously, to live by the Spirit, or to be guided by the Spirit. This means that you live a life that is connected to the Holy Spirit on a regular basis, showing our dependency and God, and by this, we know He abides in us, by the Spirit whom He has given us. — 1 John 3:24. Therefore, walk by the Spirit, and you will not carry out the desire of the flesh (Galatians 5:16). Notice that the apostle Paul doesn't say we won't have the desires of the flesh when we walk in the Spirit, but that we won't carry out those fleshly desires. When you walk, you go forward. There is a destination, a place in life where I bring God glory when I arrive. So, where do I need to be?

God made it possible for every faithful child of God to not only be in the Spirit on the Lord's Day but to Walk in the Spirit every day, and the Holy Spirit becomes the one you depend on as you go through life.

Faithful women of God have the indwelling Spirit of Christ, the Comforter who proceeds from the Father (John 1 5:26). The Holy

Spirit assists every faithful child of God in prayer (Jude 1:20) and "intercedes for God's people in accordance with the will of God" (Romans 8:27). He also leads faithful women and men into righteousness (Galatians 5:1 6—1 8) and produces His fruit in those yielded to Him (Galatians 5:22-23). Those who claim to be believers are to submit to the will of God and walk in the Spirit.

What does it mean to Walk in the Spirit? A "walk" in the Bible is often a metaphor for practical daily living. The Christian life is a journey, and only the faithful can walk it—every child of God is required to make consistent forward progress during his or her walk (2 Peter 1:5-7). The biblical norm for every child of God is that they walk in the Spirit: "If we live in the Spirit, let us also walk in the Spirit" (Galatians 5: 25, Romans 8:14). In other words, the Spirit gave us life in the new birth (John 3:6), and we must continue to live, day by day, in the Spirit.

While we walk in the Spirit, we grow daily, which enables us to yield to His control, we follow His lead, and we allow Him to exert His influence over us. Faithful children of God never resist grieving Him during our daily walk with Him (Ephesians 4:30), and when the Spirit is in control, He produces godly qualities within us, apart from the strictures of the Law (verses 22—23). Those who claim to be God's children, Eph. 5..." have crucified the flesh with its passions and desires" (verse 24), and now we walk in the Spirit (verse 25).

Faithful women and men who walk in the Spirit rely on the Holy Spirit to guide them in thought, word, and deed (Romans 6:1 1—14). They show forth daily, moment-by-moment holiness, just as Jesus did when, "full of the Holy Spirit, [He] left the Jordan and was led by the Spirit into the wilderness" to be tempted (Luke 4:1).

Every child of God should know to walk in the Spirit is to be filled with the Spirit, and some results of the Spirit's filling are thankfulness, singing, and joy (Ephesians 5:18-20; Colossians 3:16). When the faithful walk in the Spirit they follow the Spirit's lead. They "let the word of Christ dwell in [them] richly" (Colossians 3:1 6), allowing the Word of God to teach, rebuke, correct, and train them through the word in righteousness" (2 Timothy 3:16).

Their whole way of life is lived according to the rule of the gospel as the Spirit moves them toward obedience. When we walk in the Spirit, we find that the sinful appetites of the flesh have no more dominion over us.

Therefore, what it means to walk in the Spirit is to tap into the help that God has already provided for you. The more you are able to do this, the stronger you will become. The less you do this, the weaker you become. So, we must stay plugged into the Holy Spirit by way of growing in the word of God, and when we do, our walk will be fruitful, and grace will be multiplied in our lives. Therefore, from this point forward, when you think of what it means to walk in the Spirit as a faithful child of God, you don't have to treat it as if it is some mystical thing. It is far more practical than that. It should be a very normal part of your daily life for one simple reason. The Holy Spirit lives inside you. Because he does, he will give you what you need to live the life he wants. Your job is to stay plugged in, and when you do, you will truly walk in the Spirit.

Those who walk in the faith are able to declare the only benefit that we need to know... "For I know the thoughts that I think toward you, says the Lord, thoughts of peace and not of evil, to give you a future and a hope. Jeremiah 29:11. Seriously, how awesome is it that God tells us exactly what He wants to give us, and how sad is it that we soon forget this verse when things are not going as planned? So, as we continue to walk by faith, we must wait as long as it takes. God is going to do what He wants to do, no matter what. In Isaiah 46:10, God says: "I make known the end from the beginning, from ancient times, what is still to come. I say, 'My purpose will stand, and I will do all that I please.

Understanding God's authority will help us to both walk by faith and have assurance that Him to work in our lives. He may not answer right away or even give us what we think we need as we continue walking by faith, but He will provide what is best for us when it is best for us. That's for certain. Your job is to stay plugged in, and when you do, you will be in the spirit and truly walking by faith.

Chapter 6
Phenomenal Woman Healthier Forever, Happier and Beautiful Forever

For us older, mature women, never OLD, just mature LOL (laugh out loud), most of us, if not all of us anyway, believe that health and beauty have shifted from unimportant (when we were younger) to top priority (meaning right now)! You see, we now live in a youth-orientated beauty Instagram world. Every dam commercial has some pretty young thing (usually in her twenties) who IS in a commercial telling us to buy beauty products we may need, but they don't. Their skin is young, tight, and already glowing skin, so why is she in a commercial about beauty products! At their age they don't need, they don't use, they don't want or buy any of those products instead of a mature woman like me that really uses these products or you! Who is the beauty industry really trying to fool? Obviously, it works because older woman spends a whopping 2 billion dollars a year on beauty products, WOW!

To be healthy, you need to understand what is happening to your aging body. It's complicated, and so are we, but you got this: you just have to rev up or increase the care you take of yourself. You see, when we all were in our twenties, mother nature (hormones) took care of our bodies and skin. It's tight, has no wrinkles, and usually has clear completion (there are always exceptions to every rule like me; I had eczema, others acne, and others even psoriasis). Anyway, you get the picture. As young women, we are so busy with raising our families, caring for our husbands, or man same difference, and going to work full-time (with part-time jobs) that we neglect (no time) to care for our bodies, so mother nature pretty much does it for us. We're just tired; we are running, taking kids to baseball practice, dance classes, church so forth and so on. Then we have a monthly cycle, sometimes painful. Sometimes, we might even have a heavy cycle, causing us to be anemic and more tired. This is a fact; our looks, skin, and even clothes get pushed back till all we can do is put on a hat or wig or pull hair back into a ponytail and keep it moving. Feel me? Get sick? Are you kidding? This goes on and on until kids grow up and leave home and husband, well. He left and married a younger, less tired woman with no kids. Ouch! We're tired, irritated, anemic, exhausted, and the only thing on a man's mind is SEX! Am I right or what? Who has the time or money to buy any beauty products? I never did.

So, by the time you get into your late thirties or early forties, you've slowed down a little, and then you begin to see the wrinkles on your forehead, eyes, and neck really all over. You start to gain weight in the stomach area, hips and legs, upper thighs and butt, and the beautiful hair you once had is now graying some or all! What the Hell is really going on? Well, it's called life. It has caught up with you. Mother Nature left and brought menopause to replace her. No longer is your skin soft, dewy, and wrinkle-free, nope! Now your face has visible wrinkles, spots, sagging eyelids, undereye bags, and a neck like a thanksgiving turkey! Oh, Hell no! Well, all is not lost, yet we still have some fight left and weapons to use called beauty products, makeup and antiaging procedures.

These changes are due to your body changing. It no longer produces the hormones (estrogen and progesterone) like it did when you were younger. Symptoms can range from mild to severe, so get ready to deal with them. Now, you can take it like the mature woman that you are, or you can freak out and fight the process (LIKE SOME OF US DO). You get divorced, get a younger man, and become a cougar, or you can begin to take responsibility for these changes. You start by seeing your doctor and having a conversation about your hormonal changes.

Stay with me. I'm going to explain just a little about what happens during menopause since I've been through it and made it. Believe me, you will, too. During your childbearing years (20-40yrs age), your body produces your hormones estrogen and progesterone, which regulate your menstrual cycles and affect the reproductive system, urinary tract system, heart, blood vessels, bones, breast, skin, hair, mucous membranes, pelvic muscles, control cholesterol, brain, and your sexual development really these hormones do everything. These are some bad mama jammers! These hormones are responsible for the curves of our body, our tiny waists, flat stomachs, wide hips, and violaceous breasts! These hormones also help us to become pregnant (releasing female eggs) and help to regulate our moods. For most of us, anyway!

Along with our hormones doing all that they do, there are also stages of menopause, such as premenopausal, then menopause, then postmenopausal! Yes, and it occurs gradually over around 10 ito 15year span. This can start as early as your late thirties (premature menopause) or normally starts to 10 years before you actually become menopausal. Actual menopause can start at 43 up to 55 years of age. You may no longer have a menstrual cycle for up to a year and may become pregnant as well. Post-menopause occurs after the actual menopause.

The symptoms of menopause have to do with which system is affected. Remember, your body has aged and is producing less to none of those hormones anymore. You will begin to have a low sex drive due to the decreased production of estrogen in your body and decreased blood supply to the vagina, which causes dryness and painful sex for some women. This can be treated with cremes, pills, and vaginal rings. The men go through their version of male menopause, too. You are not alone. They will also slow up and not want or need the desire for sex as much.

Their symptoms include fluctuation in hormone levels, which is why you have hot and cold flashes, sleep disturbances, weight gain, and mood swings. You may experience hair thinning or loss, difficulty in concentrating, memory lapses(temporary), joint and muscle aches, headaches, racing heart, breast tenderness, night sweats, urinary urgency, emotional changes (irritability, mood swings, mild depression), dry skin, dry eyes, and mouth. You may begin to see some facial hairs (chin, above top lips), anxiety, loss of energy, lack of motivation, stress incontinency (leak urine if cough or sneeze), urge incontinence, painful urination and nocturia (nighttime urinating).

Menopause even affects your gut, which plays a major role in metabolizing estrogen by converting it into a form that makes it available to supporting organs that need it (estrogen). Menopause interrupts the natural gut process and balance. It also affects our metabolism which is just chemical reactions and process in our body that turns food into energy. If you USE more calories than you take in, it will cause you to GAIN weight. Now, if you use fewer calories, you lose weight. To boost your metabolism, you can do stuff like strengthening training and lifting weights, which burns lots of calories. Also, weight resistance bands (a stretchy item that looks like a rubber band) help build muscles. But if you Want to burn more calories than you, do aerobic exercises like walking (l do daily for 30 minutes or more), swimming, bike riding, jogging, dancing, tennis, and badminton. All these exercises help you to lose weight and stay fit and trim if done regularly, and consistently like I do (walk daily, even on weekends).

Some more symptoms of menopause include crashing fatigue. I still suffer from this as well. The symptom is due to an abrupt loss of energy. Yes, I feel tired at times and have to rest for a while until I feel less tired. And it comes upon you in a wave of exhaustion that hits you and appears to come out of the blue. The first time it happened to me, I thought I was losing my mind. It's because your body is going through huge changes that can be exhausting, and it is, trust me! I have slowed down a bit, not much, but now I cannot do the same amount of running around as I used to; you will get used to it, too. You can manage this fatigue like I do with rest periods and changing your diet, too! You will need to eat more frequently to help maintain your energy levels during the day. I'm not saying eat a full course meal which will only make you bigger weight wise and wider too, that is why the men now want younger women because they're trim and were not! But a banana, orange, peaches (can and fresh), baby carrots (delicious), grapes I could go on, but you get the picture.

I'm going to walk for 30 minutes when I get through with this paragraph.

Anyway, eat fruit or vegetables like apples (good for bowels), fruit, dried fruits, nuts, carrot or celery sticks, bananas, salads, whole grains, and protein foods like these. You're also going to need to eat more calcium for bone strength in foods like dairy products (dairy pills can be taken to combat gas or bloating), calcium supplements (pills), spinach, almonds, beans or chia seeds, also heart-healthy fats like Omega 3 fatty acids in fish can help lower your blood pressure and decrease hot flashes as well. Now, I used to be able to eat spicy foods, hot sauce, and such, but I no longer can eat them, so avoiding spicy foods, alcohol, and caffeine for these foods all triggers HOT FLASHES! And sugar and fat are another story all together. They are not your friend. Sugar alone is not good for your body. It causes your arteries to become harder, leads to higher blood pressure, inflammation, weight gain, diabetes, and fatty liver disease, along with an increased risk of heart attacks and stroke.

Along with the other negative effects sugar has, such as weight gain, it is linked to acne, increased risk of diabetes, increased risk for cancer, depression (we eat more when sad), and speeds up the aging of our skin. Too many fatty, greasy foods can also lead to a buildup of fat in your arteries, increasing your risk for heart disease, stroke, and obesity. After you age, your body does, too, and you will not be able to eat unhealthy foods like sugar and fat. It will only cause more health risks, heart disease and stroke. You do not want to be an old, old cripple trust me. I work with stroke patients, and a lot of them are depressed, miserable, unhappy, and very overweight (over 300lbs). And get very angry at staff because they choose to eat all the wrong foods, and now they can't do for themselves anymore. And people are getting younger. We had a male stroke patient, 32 years old, but weighed over 300lbs had a stroke! Yes, 32 years old, the body could not handle his overweight, his fat and sugar consumption, and it gave out! Your body cannot do its job of keeping you alive unless you work with your BODY!

Drugs, alcohol, and cigarettes are all HARMFUL to your body. The various makers of these substances don't want you to know that. You are making them BILLIONAIRES! They want you to buy this stuff and continue to use it. They do not care what effects it has on our BODIES! That is why in minority neighborhoods, McDonald's is on almost every corner, as well as Burger King, Taco Bell, and all the other fast-food chains, to make money. Ride through the wealthy neighborhoods I do, and I don't see many fast-food places, but I do see restaurants that serve quality meals. The wealthy don't serve their kids fast food or junk food like most of us do. Single mothers are too tired to cook, so they pick up food, not aware of the sugar and fat content, nor do our kids know (fat, sugar content)! Do we give our family fresh fruits and vegetables, because last time I checked, fries were not a healthy vegetable it is if you bake it though, which we seldom do? When my kids were little, I cooked meals like red beans and rice, greens, spaghetti meatballs, etc. I had no major health issues with my kids. Thank God they were healthy. I believe in holistic living, healthy food, and spiritual food that would be GOD! As adults, they won't eat red beans, greens, or spaghetti. No lie, they say they were sick of eating it growing up. I'm okay with that, but I do cook it for my grandkids, though they love it! You can't do better unless you know better. Education is the key!

And don't leave out the water in our diet; we need that too. It has many advantages; for one, it helps your body absorb nutrients, keeps your digestive tract moving, helps you feel full (eat less), and helps you stay more ALERT! When you experience hot flashes or night sweats, you lose water, so you need to replace the losses and drink more water.

Another symptom is dairy intolerance, and bloating is the one thing I hate about menopause; you see, I love ice cream! Oh, well, this is due to a domino effect in our guts or intestinal tract. You see, estrogen (female hormone) is responsible for keeping the right levels of bile and waste in our bodies. When our estrogen levels drop, then this causes bile and water levels to drop too, making our body think uh, I'm out of body water, so I must be dehydrated! Then your body responds by storing more, and more, and then more WATER, thus the bloating puffiness (darn body) in the stomach and waist area. Now you see why we have the midlife weight gain in our middle.

Then the estrogen, which also affects our bile production, causes our bodies, again, to react differently, which can cause you to digest FAT DIFFERENTLY, resulting in higher levels of GAS IN OUR DIGESTIVE TRACT. Yes, I said gas, bloating, you know what that is. But as I read this, it makes me marvel at how wonderfully made our bodies are and how people abuse them. When they mess up their bodies through drug and alcohol abuse, I get to hear all those sad stories from my patients about if I only knew and If I could have just done that differently and so forth and so on. I don't get it. If you saw what drugs did to your friend or family member, what makes you any different from them? The Devil and those portals in your MIND! It boils down to a choice, and often the Devil will persuade you to make a CHOICE WHICH you AND ONLY YOU WILL HAVE TO ACCOUNT FOR, WHICH IS SORRY, SHAME THEN DEATH AND THE LOST OF YOUR PRECIOUS soul FOREVER! If it was not precious (your soul), the Devil wouldn't be doing all he is doing; sorry, the Spirit took me there! The gas and bloating results in slowing your digestive system again, causing a domino effect causing constipation (need laxatives or stool softeners regularly). Now, you can relieve these changes by changing your diet, as mentioned earlier.

Swallowing air can lead to an increase in gas, too, and happens when you drink carbonated beverages (diet Coke, Sprite, etc.) or chew gum (Big Red, wriggles, etc.).

Getting back to menopause will change the good bacteria in your gut or digestive system, which is responsible for breaking down food. This imbalance of bacteria caused by the low hormones (estrogen and progesterone) leads to problems with your body processing food which then results in gas or farting. We can sometimes do constipation (no bowel movement in 3 or more days). Also, it can cause other minor digestive problems such as dyspepsia (which I suffer with), which affects the lower digestive tract and also causes bloating, more gas, fullness, abdominal pain, and indigestion (we can't get a break can we)! The cause of all this is still unknown (they are working on it) but is associated with excess acid, food allergies, diet, some of our medications (did you read the information sheet along with medication telling you about the side effects), stomach inflammation, NSAIDS (Aleve, Motrin) which are used for inflammation, fevers, and joint inflammation, and so forth.

Now, when you turn around 50 or so (menopause), you have a higher rate of ulcer development, increased stomach acids, bloating, and all sorts of digestive disorders. Also, bloating can cause other more serious concerns such as irritable bowel syndrome, GERD.

(gastrointestinal reflüx disease), Celiac Disease and colon cancer. Yes, you can combat all this discomfort, such as avoiding chewing gum. I did, and I don't suffer as much with gas or bloating because chewing triggers more acid enzymes to be produced, which leads to excess than dyspepsia; you get it now. Avoid carbonated drinks (coke, sprite, etc.) or drinks with that carbonation in them like fountain drinks; instead, drink more water, teas, and lemon-aids, they help digestive processes to work better and smoother.

Stay with me now; some foods trigger bloating and gas buildup as well such again, such as dairy, refined sugars, or glutens, to name a few. Try to eliminate these food items from your diet. It will reduce the bloating and gas formations. Also, try peppermint tea, which is a great way and home remedy that will help to reduce gas and settle your digestive tract. Alcohol and tobacco will also trigger bloating as well as other digestive issues, so try to avoid them as much as possible. You can also use some over-the-counter medications such as TUMS and Gas-X, to name just a few stores that have a whole shelf of medications to choose from or consult your doctor, who can prescribe you some medications. I had to go to the doctor and found out that not only did I have gas and bloating but food allergies at my age, which was causing a lot of my discomfort. So now I avoid certain foods, and my gas and bloating went away.

I'm not finished yet with symptoms caused by menopause, but INSOMNIA is a big one and a problem for me. What can I say? It is a struggle. Those old hormones can cause you problems, especially with sleeping at night, but you can get some help as well. See your doctor for these and all your menopause discomforts because there are hormone therapy options (pills, gel, patches, cremes, vaginal rings, etc.) and nonhormone therapy. For one, you can start by limiting your alcohol and caffeine intake, which can also trigger hot flashes. Eat more soy-rich foods, which can help alleviate menopause symptoms because soy milk contains phytoestrogens, which have the same chemical structure as estrogen and can increase estrogen levels in your body. Anyway, avoid naps during the daytime because, again, you won't be sleepy by bedtime. Darken your bedtime and cut off television which signals t your body to unwind and go to sleep. You will need 7-9 hours of sleep nightly, which plays a CRITICAL role In weight management. YES, I said your weight management. Because at night, you may have nighttime Cravings of high caloric-dense foods like carbohydrates. I try not to eat after 7 pm and am good at that. Also, melatonin and Benadryl) can purchase both over the counter) are useful for sleep, avoid sleeping pills, as they tend to be addictive. Also, take these sleeping medications early, like 7 pm. They tend to give you a groggy and foggy feeling in the mornings.

And weight gain in menopause should be a whole library on that stuff! It is aggravating, humiliating, and discouraging, but you can keep the weight down. I do and so can you. I do mine by avoiding carbohydrates, no fries (unless in the air fryer, and I limit it to 6 fries, no kidding), no rice, portions of pasta, or slices of bread. Again, it is a choice do you want to be FAT or SLIM. Because the choice is yours, I've been overweight, no thank you, and you get used to it. On special occasions I will eat some things but only on special occasions, my birthday, some cake etc., holidays and such. But it is a life change you choose your health. I nurse sick people who all say or did exactly what the doctor told them NOT to do, and they're paying for it with diseases, overweight, misery, and death brought on by their own negligence. Be smarter than that, PLEASE! For once, take care of YOU because Mother Nature checked out on us and left us to take care of ourselves, and that is just what I do. It's now about me and how I can take better care of myself.

Weight control is an issue after fifty and a challenge, but like me, you are up to the challenge. The first tip for slimming down for mature women is simple. Start now to limit the size or portions of your food. Instead of a big cooking spoon, take a tablespoon of something like vegetables, salad, and such. Try to eat between 1,500 to 2,000 calories a day. Yes, you can do it, I do, and once your body gets used to your diet, you won't get hungry. If you do start to be hungry, drink some tea or water or exercise. Women over age fifty gain around 2-5 pounds during perimenopause due to low estrogen levels, which in the visceral fat area (stomach) promotes fat storage and is linked to insulin resistance, type 2 diabetes, heart disease, and other health problems. Fluctuation in estrogen and progesterone can lead to us feeling hungry, and increased appetites plus fat gained during perimenopause cause us to become overweight. And not some of us, but the majority of us, that weight sneaks up on us, and before you know it, you've gained 10 pounds easily. But you can do something about it, and I do.

Reduce your carbohydrates or, like me, eliminate them all together. You don't need them that much anymore. Carbohydrates turn into SUGAR. I said sugar, so eat less and eat more vegetables, fruits, and fibre. Add more fibre to your diet, including flex seeds, which improve insulin sensitivity, more exercise, and plenty of sleep (7-9 hours a night). Add flaxseeds to oatmeal (eat more of this also) or to smoothies because they provide phytoestrogen, a plant-based estrogen that works like estrogen in our body. Eat more berries, too, like blueberries, raspberries, and my favorite, strawberries, because these stimulate collagen, which is the stuff that keeps our skin firm and fresh looking.

Start with breakfast (fruit, juice, coffee, etc.), for lunch you can have a big full-course meal (consumes most of your calories) because it helps with weight control you will burn off most of these calories this is our busiest time of the day and light dinner soup, sandwich or salad. Drink lots of water, teas, and low-calorie drinks like noncarbonated drinks, which are made with sugar substitutes (which can also cause gas). Watch the amount of salad dressing you use because a tablespoon may have 150 calories, and 4 tablespoons could have 600 calories. That's half of your calories for the whole day. I use only a tablespoon of salad dressing because of all the sugars in salad dressings. Be careful READ LABELS! Menopausal weight gain is related to one major factor: you're EATING! But it is also associated with our aging, lifestyle (sitting in front TV alone and eating), and genetic factors (no comment, but how many of us have a Big Mama in the family? That's all I'm saying about that) while the fat is increasing on us.

Plus, losing muscle mass slows the rate at which your body uses calories or metabolism.

That pesky weight gain is also due to our lack of EXERCISE! Along with our unhealthy eating habits (fast, fried, and takeout foods) and lack of enough sleep (menopause insomnia), I call it! Excess weight can increase too, especially around our middle (stomach), which also increases heart and blood vessel diseases, breathing problems (excess weight gain), and type 2 diabetes, to name a few. Weight gain also increases your risk for cancers, yes, CANCERS! This includes breast (black women have an increased rate of cancer than white women), colon, and endometrium (lining the vagina and uterus). Again, we got this. We can do something about weight gain; you are not a helpless VICTIM!

There are a lot of things you can do to help or offset your weight gain. Invest in yourself, and take your health and confidence back like I did. I am in my 60s, yet I don't look like it because I manage my weight with diet modifications, including daily walking, and it works! You have to get off the couch, put the drumstick down, and get up and get to walking, jogging, swimming, or bicycling. As you gain muscles, your body burns more calories more efficiently, which makes it easier to lose and control your weight. I have a treadmill, stationary bike, real bike, and elliptical machine, which I use daily, and I walk for 30 minutes at Work for my lunch (as I usually eat salad, sandwich, or SOMETHING LIGHT). Eat more fruit, vegetables, and whole grains, especially those that are less processed and have more fiber, legumes, nuts, soy, fish, low-fat dairy foods (yogurt, cottage cheese), and boiled eggs (carry around with me to snack on or deviled eggs). I also eat dried fruits like prunes, apricots, pineapple, and apple, all delicious and keep me from snacking on junk foods, too. Avoid a lot of red meat (it has a lot of fat, pork) and eat more chicken (not fried) and turkey meats leaner with less fat. Motivate yourself, I talk to myself, self you can do this, and I did. I have more confidence, look better, and have more energy now than I did before. I lost fifty or more pounds several years ago, and I still watch what I eat because of our slower metabolism.

Watch out for those hidden sugars, which make up to 300 calories per item, like coffee drinks from Starbucks or Dunkin doughnuts. I have them only on special occasions because they have too much sugar content, and I love coffee but make my 1 cup a day in the morning when I get up. Avoid soft drinks; all contain nothing but sugars, energy drinks (sugars), flavored water drinks (also sugars), and coffee creamers (sugars), as well as sweetened tea drinks, pumpkin, macchiato, spice, and all those flavored Coffee and tea drinks full sugar, avoid them PLEASE! Please don't eat cookies, candies, pies, cakes, doughnuts, or ice creams. All contain 300-500 calories, and that is nothing you need. It only causes weight gain, got it? Every now and then, I may crave some ice cream or cake, and I go get myself a slice of cake or ice cream for that moment, and after a few bites, I'm through; I'll throw away or give away I no longer have that craving, and I don't eat the rest. Now, belly fat is the hardest to get rid of. Get yourself a GOOD girdle. That's all I can say about that. But on the real side, the fat around the stomach is due to our low estrogen levels, which influence where fat is distributed in our bodies, so we have to help our bodies by watching what we eat, mostly unhealthy sugars, carbohydrates, and fats. We can eat more plant-based foods like fruits, vegetables and whole grains. Must eat leaner cuts of meat, more proteins, and low dairy foods. Avoid high-fat cheeses and butter, too. Eat moderate, monosaturated, and polyunsaturated fats found in fish, nuts, and certain vegetable oils. Don't forget to EXERCISE, WALK, BICYCLING, etc. Just get up and do some form of exercise each and every day that you're ALIVE! Cause when you're dead, you're DONE! This is the ma)or difference between being trim and overweight! Join a dance class, yoga class, sewing class, join a gym, meet new people and eligible men, and enjoy yourself as you lose weight. Team up with some friends and walk in the park or in the mall with the other mall walkers; they look trim and healthy!

That is a lot of information, but I'M NOT THROUGH YET! Because of our bodies being older(menopause) we have to help our bodies out by also eating more foods that contain our body hormone estrogen. Remember, our bodies no longer produce as much, which is why we have all these unwanted and unneeded symptoms, so we have to help our bodies, too. Eat more foods like soy products, tofu (high in phytoestrogens), olives, kale, wheat bran, sesame and flax seeds, and herbs (thyme, garlic, sage, and turmeric). Soy foods that contain phytoestrogens have been linked to lower cholesterol levels, improved menopause symptoms, lower osteoporosis, and certain types of cancers. Again, it's your body. You can do whatever you want to with it, but if you want to live a healthier, happier life, try some of these suggestions because they do work!

So, as we get older, never OLD, but aging gracefully, we do gain some extra weight around our middle or stomach area, to be specific, at least I did. And that is because our magnificent body tries to preserve as much hormone (estrogen) for us as it can but at a cost to us as well. The body then stores it as FAT! Yes, fat, but that is because we can no longer make this hormone(estrogen) in our adrenal glands (in the brain), so the other place it can be stored is in our peripheral fat stores (stomach area). That figure of all the places to store fat would be in our stomachs; why, Lord, why not in our butts! LOL (laugh out loud), and this is due to our insulin levels going up, so our bodies store this extra fat in this area of the stomach, which also causes us to gain weight 5-20 pounds. Our bodies can't metabolize (burn up) carbohydrates (bread, rice, fries, pasta, cake, cookies, etc., which is why I don't eat them less fat in the stomach area) anymore. Then our bodies (domino effect) overreact to our pancreas producing insulin (breaks down sugars) and stores fat. So, we have to eat the foods that our bodies now can handle (fruits, vegetables, soy products) if we want to keep our weight down. Some of us get it; we have to watch closely what we eat now, but a lot of us don't. To take better care of your body, you have to eat foods that increase your insulin levels, like vegetables, fruits, and lean meats (chicken and turkey). Watch some fresh fruits. They can be full of natural sugars; try dried fruit instead; it tastes just as good with lower caloric and sugar content.

Portion control can let you enjoy almost all foods and alcohol in moderation. Obesity is a problem in the United States and is the leading cause of Heart Disease, Breathing, and Respiratory Diseases. Extension, you get the picture. Is it clearer now to see why diet change is needed if you want to be healthy and happier? If you are single like I was several years ago, then you know that most older men don't want overweight women or women who look OLD. The man may look old, but they don't want YOU to look old and overweight and run down. Take a look at women our age and see how many are single, and if they are single, they are overweight. Trust me, if they're single and overweight, usually not married or in a relationship. If single and smaller usually have a man and a relationship too. I know I was overweight and in dysfunctional marriages, but the husbands cheated, and we never went out or anything like that. All I did was eat due to depression and codependency. I'm trying to help someone to become a Phenomenal Woman and live your best life it's a choice that only You can make. t did and am so glad I chose life, health, and love!

To continue to look fabulous like we do, we have to start taking care of our bodies better now than before. Again, that's because we're in a youth-orientated Instagram society, and looks play a major role now more than ever before. We have to manage our health and bodies, too. Don't ask me why you already read all that menopause stuff. If it's not clear, read it again: because of our decreased 'production of estrogen and progesterone, we are going through menopause and all the other changes in our bodies. The skin is a BIG one!

This is the first thing people see when they see you. It represents YOU! I hate to say it, but if your skin is not together, you will leave a bad impression of yourself. I dress fierce and sexy because that is the way I feel. Regardless of your perception of me, it is what it is. I'm not going to change for anyone, so just represent yourself. You will have to battle with your skin due to dryness, excessive for me because I have eczema. You may have skin issues, too, like psoriasis and dermatitis, but these are manageable with steroidal ointments and creams prescribed by your doctor. Bathing takes a toll on our skin as well, so you have to switch to milder, gentler soaps like Dove (my favorite), Caress, AND SO MANY MORE NOW MADE WITH COCOA BUTTER SHEA BUTTER AND SUCH TO RESTORE MOISTURE TO THE SKIN THAT BATHING REMOVES. You have to use warm water instead of hot water again because it takes less moisture from the skin. After the bath, DO NOT DRY OFF. Nope, instead, put on a lotion like Keri lotion Jerkins, then follow that will A&D ointment, Vaseline, or such to seal in that moisture. I use Keri and Vaseline, and it works like a charm for me. I no longer have dry, ashy skin. I hate to see women running around with dry-looking skin. Wow! I carry a tube of Vaseline in my purse and apply it to my hands and lips all day and after I wash my hands at work.

Now, the face is a part of your skin, too, but we need extra, extra care for that as well. I use products on my face, especially formulated for mature skin like mine. My go-to is Mary Kay; I've used it for over 10 years and LOVE it! You can choose whatever facial products you like, but it will affect how they work, how long it takes to work, and if they work. I have used dollar-store products and had no results for my skin. I used drugstore creams, cleansers, and moisturizers, and things happened again. But when I started a skin regimen with Mary Kay in about three weeks, I saw a change in my face. It was smoother and less wrinkled, so I kept using it so much that I now sell it. I believe in these products, and my face is proof that they work. I don't rely just on facial products; I use a skin brush to cleanse my skin well. Also, a skin mask, facial scrubs, and facial fillers from an anaesthetic doctor are needed.

Makeup is a choice. Everyone has what they like and dislike. I wear very little makeup because, honestly, I have never been a makeup person. When I used to wear it, my husband always commented that he didn't like it, and I agreed, so I don't wear a lot of that. However, I love Mary Kay cosmetics, Miresse lip glosses, and Mac lipsticks. I do know matte lipstick makes your lips dry out while lip glosses plump up your lips and make them look YOUTHFUL! I love my lips to be beautiful, and they do! But I also wear eyeliner, mascara, and some light eyeshadow. Makeup should enhance your looks, not make you look made-up, you know what I mean. These new makeup trends like cat eye contouring, honestly, I don't get it; why can't you look like you? God made us all beautiful. Yes, we may need some enhancements, especially as we grow older, but we don't need some of that stuff, And opinions are like assholes. Everyone's got one. I prefer natural-looking makeup for mature women. My eyelashes were thin(menopause), and I kept getting individual lashes, which further broke off my natural lashes until I hardly had any left. I saw a sign at the anthesis office on an eyelash serum called La Issue, and it is a game changer. I've been using it for 6 months and now have luscious lashes. I use it nightly, but it's pricey, but it's well worth it. My friends comment on my lashes, and I love them too. You have to have a Doctor's prescription for it because it is an eye medicine (originally used for glaucoma dry eye, but eyelashes grew long, so now used to grow eyelashes). I am becoming like a natural woman at it!

If you have wrinkles, noticeable sagging, age spots, sun damage, or acne scars, there are treatments for that, too. The doctor can resurface your skin by taking off the top layer to reveal softer, less wrinkled skin underneath. This procedure will also improve your skin texture and reduce (you won't be able to see) your fine lines by using concentrated light rays. Chemical peels are another enhancement alternative, which is just an application of acid that peels and exfoliates and gently removes dead skin cells from the top layer of your skin, leaving it looking smoother, brighter, and YOUTHFUL, HOT DOG! Also, there are Hyaluronic Acid Fillers used to reduce the appearance of fine lines and wrinkles, now plumping up and contouring your face. This procedure adds volume and fullness to your face instantly at that moment, like Juvéderm (popular with younger women as well), and is injected into your skin. There are also some new products for skincare called MEP (METHULESTRAODIOL). What this does is target collagen loss, strengthen the skin epidermis, and boost collagen production (responsible for firmness of skin). This is a new skincare technology that helps strengthen our skin's barrier and decrease estrogen deficiency. Use skin care products that stimulate collagen production (remember, collagen makes our skin firm and plump) and products that contain Vitamin C and Retinol (my superhero), which help reduce sagging skin (comes with menopause).

There is so much out there now you can choose to make us look our best. You can color your air. I hate seeing grey hairs. Now, some of us look good gray, but some of us don't. In fact, it makes you look older and listless or dull-looking. I don't look good with grey hair and choose to use Clairol my new best friend. I love hair color of reds, blonds, and such, but they destroy my hair and breaks it all the way down to my scalp, so I no longer abuse my hair. I use semi-permanent color and moisturize my hair weekly with protein packs for hair.

Usually, the hair color for mature women should be warm-toned hues. These colors make our skin tone brighter: honey blonds, bronzes, butterscotch, and chocolate browns all make you look younger with a brighter complexion. The gray color can and will wash you out and can make you look older; it really does! I now use hair greases and moisturizers, especially for DRY hair. Also, shampoos that are more nourishing, like love Shea Butter product line, for my hair, which has made it softer. I'm now letting my hair grow out naturally. No more perms, which only break off my hair, gentler products, no products with alcohol, no spritz, etc. My go-to now is lace front wigs. They look so natural, or I wear sew-ins, which allow your hair to grow and not break off. I also wear braids not often hate it because it takes a long time (4-6 hours) to sit, and I hate that. Usually wear braids in summer months only because it's so hot.

I hope this helps some of you out who have thinning hair like me, and our hair growth has slowed down too, so we have to take extra care of our hair as well. Game changers are Minoxidil, which regrows your hair. No kidding! I use it for the edges of my hair. It grew them back plus, other parts tha were thin too. I buy it from Walmart. Also, I take Biotin 20,000 units for hair growth along with Vitamin C 500mg, Thiamine, Calcium for our bones, and Multivitamin/multimineral pills. They really work wonders for your hair and body. Trust me, I take these supplements daily. My skin is beautiful thanks to Vitamin C, and I feel good most of the time due to my multivitamins.

And with your diet modifications and portion reduction, continual exercising will produce weight loss if you don't give up. You should lose no more than 2 pounds a week, and it will usually take time to get your weight down; just take your time. If exercising is not your thing, walking should be. Walk at least 30 min a day or more if you can. Bring your phone and listen to some oldies or whatever you like. Don't forget to get your rest too and do activities that make you happy. I like thrifting (going to used stores, antique stores, Goodwill, and Salvation Army stores) because I like antiques and some older clothing. I have a girl's night out with some friends and my husband, and I also have a date night. All of this is designed to keep you sociable and happy. Get your weight under control, for that will help you stay healthier. Take care of your skin and hair, too. Use friendlier products with more moisturizers for our dryness due to body changes and menopause. Looking good adds confidence and pep to your step.

I love quotes, and this one was by Mother Theresa, who was a humanitarian. She Said People are often unreasonable, illogical, and self-centred: FORGIVE THEM ANYWAY. If you are kind, people may accuse you of selfish alternative motives: BE KIND ANYWAY. If you are successful, you will win some false friends and some true enemies: SUCCEED ANYWAY. If you are honest and frank, people may cheat you: BE HONEST AND FRANK ANYWAY. What you spend years building, someone may destroy overnight: BUILD ANYWAY. If you find serenity and happiness, they may be jealous: BE HAPPY ANYWAY. The good you do today, people will often forget tomorrow: DO GOOD ANYWAY. Give the WORLD the best you have, and it may NEVER be enough: GIVE THE WORLD THE BEST YOU'VE GOT. ANYWAY, YOU SEE, IN THE FINAL

ANALYSIS, IT IS BETWEEN YOU AND GOD: IT WAS NEVER BETWEEN YOU AND THEM ANYWAY! I love this. It speaks the truth! I pray I have said something anything to inspire you to become the true phenomenal woman, you were meant to be!

Chapter 7
Dating and Domestic Violence

I keep getting women, friends even coworkers asking me, "How did you get a good man?" So, I include it in every book I write because I believe that God does and will answer prayers. If that is your desire for a good man or even a good husband like I now have, just ask God for him, like I did. Believe me, there are STILL good men and LOVE out here. You have to find it. Is it easy? Hell NO! Is it possible? Yes, and the Bible says I can do ALL Things through Christ who strengthens me Philippians 4:13. I believe this with all my heart, and it is one of my favorite verses as well.

Getting back to dating, there is no right or wrong way to date. It just depends on what you want, like, and even desire. I have spent days, weeks, and hours listening to YouTube, mostly Stephen.

Speaks, and the others, too, on dating tips. My interest is in what men want and desire in a woman to date or even marry, so I can enlighten you. Who better to ask than a man? Sometimes Stephen Speaks, or most of the time, he hits the nail (dating) right on the head; there is some advice I disagree with, so again, I'll write about some ways you can date. I also asked my husband, his male friends, and so on about women and what they look for in a woman to date and or marry. So hopefully, this chapter will be a help to you.

Technology is so huge now people use computers for everything, including advice, instructions, lots for entertainment, medicine, and sociable. It even replaced elementary education, which happened during the pandemic. Schools were closed, and learning was shifted from the classroom to the living room, bedroom, and kitchen anywhere they had a space and a computer hookup.

Technology is replacing relationships or rather affecting them because now the number one way people look for love is on the internet. I am not an advocate for internet dating, but many others are. Now, young, middle-class, older, rich, and poor use internet sites to hook up with someone. I am in my sixties I am not into the Internet dating scene at all. I never dated on the internet, and I don't think I ever will, but still it does exist. I like old old-fashioned way of boy meets girl, boy likes girl, boy marries girl: you get it the old-fashioned way, but time changes, and we have to do the same or get lost in the shuffle. This is the times we're living in now, so you have to, at times go with the flow.

So, for dating, the number one sites for mature, older (over fifty) people are Bumble, E-Harmony, Silver Singles, Match, and Our Time, but there are literally hundreds of sites to choose from .I'll let you know some of the good things about online dating as well as the bad ones. Let's start with the good ones. I looked up how many mature people actually use dating sites, and I was surprised that 1 in 10 adults use online dating because it is said to widen your search and reach people in every area (including rural areas) and anywhere you can use the internet. This will expand your dating pool to different kinds of people, also allowing you to connect with more diverse people (other cultures and nationalities), even people you would not otherwise cross paths with. Maybe you wanted to date an Italian man or an Oriental man; the skies were the limit. There are a lot of interracial dating now more than ever before. You can meet people different from you that can challenge you. You can weed through the profiles to see what it is a certain person you may be interested in or want the same things you want in a relationship be it a long-term relationship or just a short fling. You can date as many as you want as often as you want without having to worry about being rejected. It's ideal for shy people, nerdy people, and people who are not sociable. If you have a preference like red, blonde, or something of this nature, you can put that in your profile. If you like big biceps, broad shoulders, whatever your preference just list on your profile as well. If you meet someone who is not to your liking, you just unfriend them on your site (safety feature). Now, 40% of people say they matched the personality and were compatible with people they met online.

It is comfortable to use (anywhere in your home, sofa, bed, office, work, restaurant, any and everywhere you happen to be), especially if you use a mobile (cell phone) app. It is a fact that 2/3 of couples started out online on a dating site; you don't need to dress up or anything like that; you just sit down and open your phone or computer and start chatting with someone on a dating site. Too convenient if you ask me, but that's my two cents! You can chat online anytime without a commitment to these online people. You can do it anytime and anywhere. You don't have to go out, meet people and sit acrossfrom someone you now have options. You don't have to buy a new dress, new shoes, nothing just chat online. You meet these people online without having to see them, and it's socially accepted. So, there are a few of the good points about online dating.

Now a few of the bad things about online dating. I don't like it and have not tried it. I know family and friends who have tried it and loved it; some got married some did not. A few were even in a long-term relationship. One person I know met her husband online and ended up moving to Texas. They're still married and have two kids. So, for some, it works well. I'm just not a fan of the internet. People online will give a lot of false personal information about themselves. They will also post pictures of someone else they know or a picture of them 20 or 30 years ago. I had a coworker after a divorce decided to try online dating. She met a trucker who owned his own truck, so he said. Anyway, they met up at a restaurant. She kept seeing this man wandering around looking for someone; he finally came up to her and introduced himself as her date. He did not look like the picture at all. He looked worse, she said. He had a belly like Santa and was bald. That was not the picture on his profile. That picture was of him 20 years ago, neither the less they did not see one another after that disaster of a dinner, it was silent and awkward the whole evening!

No, thank you! I want to see what I'm getting: no smoke screens(computer) or hiding from your looks. To me, there's a reason why they want to date online, and I bet it has a lot to do with their looks. Your appearance should not be the ONLY reason you date someone, but truth be told, it is an important fact, especially if you are over 50! Yes, older mature women tend to be overweight (menopause) due to sedimentary lifestyles (sitting in front TV eating) and not exercising and not staying fit. That is the number one reason men say they date younger women; older women look OLDER! Again, we're now in a youth-orientated Instagram society; looks are everything now more than ever before. That is the reason I wrote the book Phenomenal Woman because older women have so much to offe besides our looks. Some of us just got stuck and need a little help, and I pray this book will help and inspire you to get it together as I did! It is not easy being older, tired, menopausal, overweight and lonely! It causes some of us to be targets of someone trying to take advantage of us. Mostly toxic and dysfunctional men. Please don't fall for their tricks. Get it together and get some counseling, fight the codependent demons and get your life, joy, and health back from the DEVIL!

For some people, online dating is very frustrating and, after a while, no longer fun or interesting. You may attract predators or people who catfish. That happened to a coworker of mine. She cash app a guy online 500 dollars to come visit her (strange) and never heard from him again after she sent him that money. That was a romance scam, and yes, they do that stuff online, too. I also heard an advertisement from AARP ABOUT DATING for older people and shame! The online person will ask for gift cards of hundreds of dollars so they can come and visit you. Hell no! Some of the people online may be shallow, you may attract the wrong kind of men (narcissists, they're online too, looking for YOU), and some lack serious intentions and just want to have sex. I had another coworker date someone online, and after three months, they met and later ended up sleeping together. The next morning, she told him she was HIV positive, and she understood if he did not want to see her again. They used protection, but what if he hadn't? This would be a different kind of ending (death).

Some coworkers tried online dating and said that you don't feel any kind of connection like you do when you meet someone in person. I say if you look good, weigh under control, eat right, look right, and smell good. No heterosexual man will be able to RESIST! Try it and see, and you can also do both online and in person but you've got to go out to meet Mr. Right. He is not going to come knocking on your

DOOR! If you're waiting for that to happen, you may be dead! And the costs of online dating are not cheap, especially if you use multiple dating sites, ouch! You can meet someone who is too sexual with you or insults you. One coworker was supposed to be matched with her online person. The site said the algorithm matched them, but they were opposites and did not see each other at all. Some people online outright lie about what they do, what they have, and so forth. People do a lot of trying to impress. They go as far as to rent expensive cars and even homes to try to impress you, which are all LIES and DECEITFUL! No thanks, that's why I like to see what I'm getting, and the men do, too! Some people use online dating because they have not had any success with traditional dating in the past. I read another quote that said A woman that trusts no ONE now once trusted someone TOO MUCH! SO, SO TRUE!

Something else I read is that men are encouraged by friends and coworkers to use online dating services, while women are urged by their kids and family to use online dating services. How interesting. Women use it as a tool to ease back into a relationship, while men use it to jump back into a relationship following a divorce or the death of a partner or spouse.

Do you wonder what a man over fifty is looking for in a woman? Well, after watching YouTube, reading articles, and interviewing my husband and his friends, I believe I have some, if not all the things older men are looking for in a woman. Older men or men over fifty look for certain qualities in a woman. Some like younger women because they may be less damaged or broken, if you want to call it that. And that's because they have not lived as long as we have or been in toxic relationships like we have to or have baggage. But then these older men have to be able to gather keep up with young women. Does he have the finances that she may want and can keep up with her lifestyle? One time, while I was out with my husband, he saw an old friend of his who had never been married but was recently married to a 30-something-year-old (he was in his fifties). Of course, she was beautiful, had an hourglass shape, had no kids, and such. I was not intimidated because I looked good, and I am a confident, beautiful black woman who makes no mistakes about that. Younger women look better than a lot of us do because they are young!

Younger women tend to keep up with their appearances more, mostly due to their hormone progesterone, estrogen, and youth. We no longer produce our hormones, and as a result, we may have added weight on us, wrinkled faces, gray hairs, and so forth and so on. Be honest some of us over fifty want a relationship if we're single but look torn up from the floor up. Our hair is gray or graying, we have our gut hanging over our pants or protruding out visibly in our clothes, we have become couch potatoes, and we do no Rind of any physical activity except working our jowls (eating). You get or rather see the big picture. But we've got to do better if we want to be happy and healthier. Face it, you may be rich, but if you're sick and spend all your time and money on doctors, private duty nurses, or in and out of a hospital, how long will you be able to keep someone special in your life? Money is not the answer! Longevity, but your health is, people are actually living longer thanks to medical advances, new medications, new surgical procedures, and such. Women are living to over 81 years of age, while men will live over 76 years of age.

Some women let themselves go, and I know some, and I'm sure you do, too. Can you picture someone now? I know I can. I had a coworker who had a moustache, no lie. Her husband left her and married a younger woman, no kidding. Another coworker and I tried to explain to her the reason she should reflow her moustache, but she would not. I still can't figure out the reason except she was broke and suffered from some sort of codependency or traumatic rape, abuse, or such. Once you've been sexually assaulted, you change; it does something to your mind. I know because I am a rape victim, too, and it stayed with me for all of my adult life. But I got counseling, which can and did change my life. Thank you, Lord!

Let's start with your appearance, which is a big thing. Even if you're younger, in your 30s or 40s, you still have to dress attractively and have confidence and, let me add, smell like a rose (or any fragrance). It draws men like honey draws bees; they love a good-looking, good-smelling, beautiful attractive woman. No man, and I do mean no man, will be able to take his looks off you when you step in any place hair l Oking fly, smelling good, and dressed girl because that is how I present myself. If you're not sure how to dress? They have services on the internet that send you clothes suited and match for you or like me, get your adult daughters, adult nieces, etc., to hook a sister that would be you up.

I have daughters, and all of them dress beautifully, and I get them to hook me up, too. One of my daughters does my hair, another my clothing, and the other one my accessories, and yes, it is that serious. You have to have pride in your appearance, or you will be alone for the rest of your life. Trust me, that was me before I got my divorce. I had no style; plain clothing did not really have a clue because I was broken. You're going to have to spruce up your clothes and your wardrobe and buy some new shoes, dresses, etc. Please don't pull out some 40-year-old shoes you wore 20 years ago and expect to attract a man. It's not going to happen. Give those old shoes and clothing to the Goodwill or Salvation Army and get a tax deduction as well.

You're going to need to do some transformations to be competent to get a man in this day and time, trust me, for that is exactly what I did. I asked some coworkers about their shoes, and they got them, as well as their clothes. They hooked me up with some online clothing sites, so I checked them out, like Shoe Dazzle and Fashion Nova. Try other sites as well or go shopping in the mall and get some advice from the saleswoman. They will help you to accessorize your outfits and tell you the truth about your looks as if they look good on you or not; this is not the one for you. I had all flat shoes or a little heeled shoe, long old-timey dresses, outdated pants and tops. High heels and stilettos make your legs look amazing while adding style to your clothing. If you can't walk in heels like me, practice

wearing them at home. Put them on while you cook, do housework, etc., until you are comfortable wearing them out somewhere. I started wearing mine to the store, movies, and church. Until now I can dance in them wobbly you hame it. If you are determined to do something, trust me where there is a will, there is a

WAY! My daughter told me, "You look a mess and will not be able to get a man," and she was right: You're going to have to re-invent your appearance if you want to date at this time and day. It's not hard to do, and It is fun. Trying on different outfits, buying new jewelry, purses, whatever, after a while, you will get the hack of dressing to impress. I look at books, magazines as well and other women while I'm out. Now, everybody will not be glamorous, but you can make some much-needed improvements to your looks. Try some microblading of your eyebrows, and if you don't know what that is, there is still hope for you!

How about your smile? Is it dazzling? If not, this is the time to visit your dentist. If you have missing teeth or decayed teeth please get it taken care of like me. My teeth were yellow from years of coffee drinking, which I still do, but I got Veneers an overlay on my teeth, which are white, and now my smile is beautiful. There are so, so many alternatives to dental care, and it looks like partial plates, tooth implants for missing teeth, and so forth. But you must visit your dentist regularly, especially as we age, to avoid tooth loss and gum diseases. How does your breath smell? Keep some mints for those occasions when your mouth is not fresh.

What about your hairdos? Are they outdated, and do you need some coloring? Again, visit a professional hairdresser to take care of your hair or, like me, buy a lace front wig. Ooh, I love them; I have all sorts of different colors and styles. Long, short, blonde, red, black, brown and platinum. Coloring breaks my hair off, so now I'm growing out my hair naturally and wearing lace front wigs instead or sewins too. In other words, spend your money to improve your looks for once in your life like me! You'll be amazed at how good you will look, feel, and act very confident and sexy! Once you take care of your appearance, it's time to go slay!

Once I got my looks together and built up my self-worth and self-esteem, I became confident and felt like a beautiful, phenomenal woman for the first time in my whole life. This is true, but sad to admit. All because I have been damaged, broken, and codependent all my life. But I'm making up for it now! Several times when I was out with my husband, I'm assuming I looked pretty good because I was hit on by a person. One person offered to buy me something; we (my husband and I) were at a play, and this was intermission. I declined nicely and stated I was with someone. This person offered to buy us both something, so you see, looks are very important because you will attract people like a magnet. Again, no one can resist a good-looking, good-smelling woman at no time, nowhere. They may be with someone, but they will still look and appreciate your appearance. I don't care who you are with; your confidence and good looks will make people immediately notice YOU! Again, we were out (husband and l), and at a small concert, one of the band members offered to buy me something again. I told them I was with someone; however, this time, they did not want to buy him something, just me again. Your look must be on point, so get inspired to look your best and improve your health, which will improve your self-esteem, boost your confidence, make you feel good about yourself and make you want to keep up your appearance. And I still get that response from people. My husband, it doesn't seem to bother him. He just keeps it moving. I, on the other hand, am amazed, but I feel so good, healthy, and happy! I am too old to lie. These are all true events that happened to me. I'm still blown away by the compliments that I receive.

Older men are looking for someone special to be in a long relationship (marriage too) with or to date. These men look for women who are smart, intelligent, and confident. A dumb blonde (old saying) just won't do anymore and is not an option. The woman should be able to communicate her wants, needs, and likes and respect his boundaries. If these men have grown kids and even grandkids, they want someone who can appreciate that this man has these types of relationships and honor them as well. These men want a woman that they can be in her and her kid's lives too. He wants an adventurous woman and one who likes to travel. She should also have substance be his equal, not act like his mother (he may already have one of those). He is looking for a woman who is fun, honest, loving, laughs and, enjoys life, values practicality over flare substance over glamour. They want strong women with their own resources and money. She doesn't want you to spend up his savings or credit cards and doesn't want someone who needs him to take care of her financially. She should have her own money and credit at this time in her life (over fifty). These older men are looking for a woman who is sexually active and likes different things in the bedroom. A woman who is open-minded to trying different things intimately. They love a feminine woman who flirts and is open and honest, too; they're too old for playing mind games. They love romantic and spontaneous women who are good kissers. So, pucker up and get ready for some hot kissing, get my drift? Be sure you're wearing that glossy lipstick or lip gloss, which makes your lips look so good, and red lipstick makes your teeth look white!

Older men look for women who are playful, imaginative, compassionate, yet sensitive at the same time. They look for women who are nonjudgmental and trustful and show key attributes they value and are compatible with their lifestyle. She has to be able to respect his time and space, act mature and carry herself well.

One of the main reasons why you may have been unsuccessful in dating is you are codependent and keep hooking up with the crazy ass DYFUNCTIONAL and TOXIC men! And yes, they are crazy. The condition is called NPD OR Narcissi Personality Disorder, and it is in the mental health guidelines along with the treatment. What? You didn't know these men are crazy and abusive, especially if you're codependent t00! I will NEVER EVER again get involved with a crazy ass dysfunctional man ever again. I lost so much money, time, self-worth, my self-esteem, to name a few, being married to this type of man. But I was codependent and did not know any better till I had counseling and rededicated my life to GOD! All I can say is, OH MY GOD, they are really crazy. It is a bonified mental condition called Narcissi Personality Disorder (NPD)! Look it up. Google and see for yourself because that was what I did; go on YouTube and watch all the stuff about it. Trust me, your eyes will really open WIDE!

There are visible signs of narcissi men I dated. A few trusted me before I GOT MARRIED. I kicked them to the curb when the craziness came out because, eventually, their mask will slip when they get comfortable with you. I look for the crazy, dysfunctional men to avoid them like they look for us to ruin us! One guy didn't want me to wear V-neck tops and didn't want my bust visible. The other one didn't want me to wear short dresses. He wanted me to wear long dresses. Both these jokers I kicked to the curb. I liked them, but NO ONE Controls ME OR PICKS MY WARDROBE EITHER. Next! I do not tolerate these types of men. I've been there and done that all my life no more. The buck stops here. You have to be assertive and let these jokers know that you mean business, and you got to keep it moving, oh yeah, NEXT! I don't have to deal with their foolishness, and nor should YOU!

Some signs of dysfunction in men will be hard to detect because they, like chameleons, can change in a flick of your eye, but if you know what to look for, you will be able to spot them.

They are usually charming, so charming it's very noticeable if you are skilled like me at picking up the phoney act of being charming. They are full of compliments, too; they use thick like syrup type of compliments (that's a sure clue). I've had them kiss my hand or the palm of my hand as I look at them crazy! I can take "you look nice "or "you're very pretty or attractive" compliments, but when they are overboard with the compliments, that is a RED FLAG for me.

Their hallmark sign of dysfunctional personality disorder is the grandiose sense of importance. They live in a fantasy world that supports their delusions of grandeur, and they need constant, and I do mean constant, praise and admiration. This reminds me of D. Trump and C. Mansion, the cult leader and former President of the United States. They were narcissistic men and crazy as hell, too. The mansion had followers murder seven or more wealthy people because he was not wealthy and targeted people who were. He brainwashed his followers, and they killed for him. D. Trump orchestrated a gathering that turned violent, and his followers tried to tear up the White House (in 2020), and several deaths occurred as well. Can you see the big picture? They are crazy, and eventually, the craziness comes out.

These types of men have some twisted sense of entitlement (feel it's owed to them everything they desire or want) and exploit other people without feeling guilty or shameful about doing this. Now that is just plain sick and twisted! These men often dismiss, demeaner you, intimidate you, bully you, and belittle you constantly. They have an unrealistic sense of superiority (again, it sounds like D. Trump). My ex-husband had the nerve to say I was stupid, and he was the one with the 7th-grade education. I had a BSN in nursing, so belittling me made him feel good about himself. See, that's how it works; they belittle YOU to Cover up for their own shortcomings. Again, sick and twisted. My ex-husband would threaten me and even choke me if I disagreed with him. Yes, they will physically and mentally abuse YOU, but that is not LOVE again. It's codependency MASQUERADING as LOVE! Because these men don't and can't love you, they love themselves. They're in love with their inflated self-image because it lets them void their deep feelings of insecurity, SHAME, AND SELF HATRED! Yes, they hide from the truth. They're nothing, and you're SOMETHING! They hide from the truth like little "BITCHES!" The truth will. Set you and me free. So, it takes a lot of work to keep their overinflated ego going. They need you and me to constantly tell them how great they are (sounds like D. Trump, doesn't it), howsmart, how manly, and so forth and so on. You get the big picture!

A lot of these narcissi men are into all sorts of different sexual relationships, too, such as the popular one called dominance and submissive (D&S). The biggest concept is that one person, usually the male, dominates (that figures) another human being, and they do whatever without question what they tell them to do. We're adults so I'm just giving my opinion about this subject. They sell all this stuff for this type of foreplay or whatever it is on the internet or in adult stores. These men can beat them with chains, tie them up with rope or twine, gag their mouths, cover their eyes with blindfolds, and demand them to perform some sort of sexual acts with them, and or they also can be with group people. I'm not approving or disapproving of anything an adult does with their life or their body, but I will say that this body was made by God; it is a temple of the Holy Spirit 1 Corinthians 6: 19 and like Mother Theresa said, in the final analysis, it is between you and God. I'm just saying this does not look to me to be LOVE!

Don't tell me you didn't see the movie 50 Shades of Grey. Well, that might be a movie to see. It was interesting, to say the least. So, in this movie, this rich white man meets this younger college girl and supposedly falls in love with her and teaches her this dominant and submissive relationship taught to him by his mother's best friend (unknown by his mother). In one scene, the man had a room in his house with all this bondage equipment in it: whips, chains, the whole nine yards. He tells the young woman to go in the corner and kneel on her knees until he tells her to get up. So, she is in a corner facing the wall on her knees for so many hours, then he comes in and whips her with a whip, ties her mouth and wrist, beats her ass then has sex with her. Hell to the no. No man is going to tie me up, beat my ass, and call that love that is some Devil and portals in your mind stuff. I've been abused. It's physically and mentally painful, further degrading your self-esteem and self-worth. It is a tactic used to CONTROL YOU! God does not ordain sick or twisted relationships, but the Devil does. Anyone, I mean man, woman, mom, dad, sister, or brother, who hurts you in any way is either mentally sick, ignorant, or they don't love or care about you and most of the time themselves either. This is not someone you should be around. They need some sort of help! And you do, too, if you allow it!

In narcissi men, if you notice these types of patterns of self-centred, arrogant thinking, lack of empathy (your mom just died, so what), and no consideration for YOU or anyone else, look out! This should be A RED FLAG! These narcissi men can even be described as cocky, manipulative, demanding, selfish, and patronizing. Just be careful. That type of behavior is not Cute. It's cunning because their/ plan is to CONTROL YOU! That is always the plan: total DOMINANCE and CONTROL! Some of these sick men have a dominant lifestyle. Some of us may be smart and pick up on these behaviors, but if you're codependent, you will not because I didn't until counseling and GOD! They give you AT FIRST want you long for "LOVE!" They are kind, considerate and thoughtful. My ex-husband, before we got into a relationship, bought me candy and flowers, we went to the park, on trips, you name it. They practice these behaviors for a living, they study us, and they know what to do to get to YOU! After several months of catering to me, he slowly changed; the mask slipped, or rather, he took it off. They can only wear the mask for so long then the real behavior and crazy personality come out! I should have left then, but codependency would not let me. I was broken.

They will begin to isolate you from your family and friends because they can tell you about his crazy ass (try toxic and dysfunctional man). He can't chance that happening, so he will make you choose him; he'll tell you lies about your family like 'your mother doesn't like me 'or 'your father talks badly to me' and other stupid things to rattle you. Then he'll tell you that you're going to have to decide whether you want to be with him or your family:' Yes, he will want you to choose a side. So, you are caught in the middle. Because you have no self-esteem or self-worth, you choose the loser (dysfunctional man). You lack boundaries and keep looking for acceptance from him, but you'll never get it, trust me. Been there, don? That and it never happened; my ex-husband made me choose between him and my own kids. They never liked him because of the way he treated me and them too. He was rude and obnoxious to them, and they knew he was ignorant and dysfunctional. I, however, was broken and did not have a clue! As they grew up, they moved out, went to college, and got their own places, but the effects of that abusive relationship have hurt my relationship with them for years after. They don't understand your codependency and all that it is. Hell, you don't understand it either. But after counseling, I could see what it was, and I talked to them about it as well.

If any of this stuff sounds like your man, husband, or boyfriend, then something is wrong; get HELP! These men are very, very sensitive to any type of criticism, disagreements, or perceived slights, which in their twisted mind is a personal attack on them if you say something like "you are always late in picking me up from work" (they don't work, drop you off at work early every day, and late to pick you up every day) they get mad, curse you out, or they'll just sulk and not talk to you. So, not to have to go through all that we avoid any and everything that can upset them and make them go off! But he has to be dysfunctional (RED FLAG) WHEN HE GETS UPSET AT You when you call him out on something! GET OUT! Girls, save your sanity and get some counseling, please!

They really think they are unique and special, and they'll have you thinking that stuff, too. They only want G to associate with other important and high-status people because it makes them feel good about themselves and their overinflated ego. Remember, under that exterior is a scared little boy who lacks self-worth and self-esteem, just like YOU! But because he is a man, he wants you to praise him, admire him, and constantly do it, too. They look for admiration all the time and look for situations and things to brag about. My ex-husband had a trucking business, which I helped him acquire, and he bragged about that ALL THE TIME! He was able to acquire two trucks, and he hired two drivers, so he supervised them all day (he didn't have to drive a truck anymore) and just bragged about his business.

These guys also make up fantasies about how successful they are, how special they are, and all sorts of bull about, you guessed it, THEM! These fantasies protect them from feelings of inner emptiness and hurt, so anything that contradicts them is ignored. Anything, and I do MEAN anything, that threatens that fantasy will be met with RAGE, so you learn to tread lightly and or carefully around his fantasy and reality. Don't try to burst that bubble, or you may be punished physically or verbally or both. Tñese men need CONSTANT (not sometimes or every now and then but constant) food for their sagging egos, so they surround themselves with you and anyone else who will cater to their obsessive craving for this affirmation of their brilliance supplied by usually You (all the time). My ex-husband talked so much about his truck, the money he made, how great he was till I got sick of him and those trucks. I was depressed and miserable and ate food for comfort, which made me gain weight up to 250 pounds (mJl heaviest)! My blood pressure went up. I was then diagnosed with hypertension. I was in my early forties.

I looked torn up from the floor, and it was very much damaged and broken. Again, my family and friends tried to get me to get counseling, but I was resistant. I believed this man loved me, fooled again. It was codependency masquerading as LOVE!

I thought that after all I did for him, he would show me some sort of appreciation, too; NOPE! That's how you know he's narcissi because if you have the nerve to ask for something, any little thing prepare to be met with aggression, outrage, or the cold shoulder. The nerve of you asking for something! You'll learn never to do that again. Remember, your needs WILL NOT be met with a narcissus man, only HIS!

Codependent women are attracted or drawn to narcissi men because, again, they are CHARMING, and some can be very magnetic (Manson and Trump), to say the least. They'll promise you the MOON, STARS, and everything else to get you to be with them. Why do you think they approach you? You didn't go up to him. Your self-esteem is almost nonexistent anyway. They're looking for women who lack self-esteem and self-worth, so you will be an obedient admirer, not a partner, in this relationship.

Your ONLY VALUE to him is to tell him how great he is and to prop up his unsatiable EGO!

We're attracted to narcissi men because they have what we lack: confidence, their loftiness, and the weaker and more fragile our self-worth and self-esteem, like mine were then, the more seductive the allure of a narcissi man. All I can say is the Devil has his hand in it because these types of men are toxic, and the Devil wants to destroy YOU as he takes your soul. Yes, your soul. The Devil will cause you to be attracted to a narcissistic man. He'll get you in a sexual, sadistic, and kinky relationship with threesomes and all sorts of twisted sexual habits along with drugs and alcohol until he destroys you, your body, and your mind. And the Devil targets us, codependent women with fragile self-esteem and self-worth, because he knows he can send a narcissi man to destroy you and perform acts to further lead you to destroy your soul and salvation. You then self-medicate by drinking alcohol (numb pain), further destroying your body, destroying your liver and pancreas, drugs further destroying your body (liver, pancreas, heart, to name a few) until death like Whitney Houston, her daughter, Rick James (heart failure from drugs) and so many other people who have killed themselves intentionally or accidental the Devil still had a hand in it his intention was to ruin their lives and their soul which he accomplished.

That is another reason why there is so much human trafficking of mostly underage young girls. Usually, these girls are runaways with no family ties (abusive, drugs, single parent, alcohol like my environment growing up), so these men pick them up and sell them to other men for sex. These young girls get caught up in something. They have no clue how they got into it or how to get out of neither. I am blessed GOD sent angels to watch over me; I never did drugs, alcohol, or anything of that nature. I grew up in the church. I knew and loved God, but because of my home environment (my mother and grandmother were alcohol), I became broken and codependent all my entire adult life. These narcissistic men are predators. They lure young girls in with kindness, buying them stuff, feeding them so forth, until they gain control of these unfortunate young girls. Again, this is all due to the Devil. Do you think any decent God-fe man would enslave young girls and sell their bodies for a profit? Of course not!

These narcissi men will lie, manipulate, hurt, and disrespect others and you too! Your feelings, ants, and needs will! NEVER, EVER be addressed, NEVER. That is how you know he's dysfunctional and toxic; your. Don't make excuses for their bad behavior or minimize the hurt and pain he is causing you. He will not change EVER. Get OUT of that toxic relationship li e I did better late than NEVER. They will never see you, hear you, only recognize you as someone who exists outside of their NEEDS (again, it comes down to everything being about HIM). He will go through your mail and your phone, listen and eavesdrop on your conversations on the phone, and then will ask you who you are talking to. Yes. He crosses all your boundaries, that is, if you have any at all, since you're keen and codependent. He wants and demands total CONTROL. And they also play sick games like gaslight you m you   u t your judgement) or love bomb (flattery and a migration) when he feels you're trying to break away or leave his ass! All I can say is, like Rev. Clay Evans says, I am truly blessed as 00k back over my life. I could have been dead, on drugs, or an alcoholic like my mother, and I don't know why I'm not, except I have a TESTIMONY. Jesus.!

NarciSsi men are dysfunctional and toxic, not to mention they are plain crazy. I will never understand how the Devil uses some people to harm other people. It's crazy, but it is called LIFE, and these individuals are out there, but you've got to get healed of your codependency and seek GOD; this is your only protection. Trust me, I know firsthand! These men can be predators, sadistic like Jefferey

Epstein was trafficking young girls in his private jet all over the world. They usually tend to be abusive. That's how they keep you in line (obeying everything they say) and keep you afraid of them (l was). This is not a black-or-white thing. It crosses all cultures and lines, but it is very much prevalent in poor black neighborhoods. We black people find it hard to trust the police (most of them tend to be prejudiced toward blacks), our community calls us a snatch (old saying snitches get stitches, which tends to be true), and we usually have some sick sort of loyalty to our black men who beats you! We're broken, and a lot of us grew up with violence in our neighborhoods and homes. I saw a lot of it when I grew up because my mother and \grandmother fought all the time because they were alcoholics. And if we do call the police, we are pressured by his family or friends as well as him to drop changes. He'll NEVER do it again. He learned his lesson this time for the hundredth time! Really!

We stay in abusive relations because, number one, we're broken, dysfunctional ourselves, and codependent. We have convinced ourselves that we love him (Codependency masquerading as love re ember), we're isolated from our family and friends (he cut that at the beginning of the relationship), he takes care and holds all the money, you're mentally, physically and psychologically abused and threatened all the time. Wow, what a horrible existence, yet that is how I lived most of my adult life. After I got so tired of being miserable, unhappy, and torn up from the floor, my family and friends interceded and got me to divorce him and get some counseling. Thank You, Jesus, for my family and friends!

Well, the statistics are ALARMING; I was upset. I did not know it was this large percentage of women who are STILL being abused and STILL in those abusive relationships! For black women, 4 in 10 BLACK women are abused physically and mentally, and 20% of black women are also raped in their lifetime.

Another flack is that women are 3 x times more at risk than any other race of women For USE and the leading cause of death of black women between ages 15-35. Women ARE killed at a rate of 4.4 per 100,000 people. Black women are at greater risk of being killed by their partners than any other race. If you are in this horrible, horrible relationship, OUT and get some help, there is help. National Domestic Violence   - 00-799-723. There are STILL women in these kinds of relationships, and I am so upset about it, but know this: YOU ARE NOT ALONE! You are not to BLAME!

YOU DON'T DESERVE to be abused EVER! BY NO ONE EVER!

Leaving this type of relationship is tough for many women because of several factors; for one, you are isolated from family and friends (he severed those relationships). Two, you are beaten psychologically and physically, financially controlled (he has to give you money, and he penny-pinches that), and are threatened on a daily basis by him.

Being in an abusive relationship is very stressful. Why do we stay? These men play mind games and tricks, I like to say. They do stuff like accuse you of cheating on them or being disloyal! My ex-husband accused me of sleeping with my minister, oh yeah, and the mailman. He went as far as to sniff or smell my panties for, I guess, the odor of semen. My ex-husband would follow me in his truck since I did home health nursing, so he said he was just trying to keep me safe! Bull!

These toxic and dysfunctional men will make you feel worthless and hurt you by physically hitting you, beating you, choking, or even kicking you. I have experienced hitting and choking by my ex-husband. All of this is done in an attempt to intimidate and bully YOU! He will also go as far as to threaten to harm you, your kids, family, or friends if he doesn't get what he wants from YOU. I was watching an old clip of Oprah, who was interviewing this woman, Carolyn Thomas, whose boyfriend, Terrance Kelly (of 8 years), killed her mother and tried to shoot her face off with a double barrow shotgun on December 5, 2003! My heart ached; that could have been me or even YOU! She lost her mother and the life she had before this tragedy. The boyfriend is in prison for life, and his reason for doing this horrific act is that he smoked some type of cigar laced with some sort of drug. The Devil!

Please don't get stuck in an abusive relationship because of confusion, guilt or selfblame https://www.verywell.com. The only thing that truly matters is YOU and your SAFETY! You are not to blame (stop beating up on yourself) for being battered or abused or mistreated it is not your fault! You are not the CAUSE of your partner's abusive behavior; YOU deserve to be treated with RESPECT. You deserve to be SAFE and have a HAPPY life. Your kids also deserve to be safe and happy too! Your abusive partner will NEVER CHANGE! Abusers need some help something is WRONG with them they have deep emotional and psychological problems (more than likely stemming from childhood or adulthood). Only with some therapy, and co they take responsibility for their behaviors instead of blaming you for their dysfunction. When you continue to stay with an abuser, you're reinforcing and enabling their behavior. You are not helping these abusers. You're only PERPETRATING the PROBLEM! Ft my ex-husband several times, but he would always beg me and convince me to come back. He would that same day continue the abusive behavior like nothing had happened and like I had never left. My ex-husband never changed his abusive behaviors, and after 14 years, I was finally tired. I was DONE! This particular day, he blacked my eye over something trivial. I can't even remember what it was, but the next day, to put makeup on and went to work as nothing happened, and I never came back. I left EVERYTHING because my family convinced me to leave the state and move out of town to Georgia

You Lord. I met my husband, and the rest is history! If I have said anything to help you leave an abusive relationship, please do. There is now help in domestic laws, shelters for you and your children, free legal help with divorces, and so much more please get some help if you are in this type of relationship! The only one who can help you is YOU! And GOD (prayer is the key; faith unlocks the door)! You can't do better unless you know better!

Chapter 8
Conclusion

I once read a quote from Colin Powell that said the greatest gift given to him by his parents was their unconditional love and values, which they not only taught but, most importantly, lived! Also, their importance in hard work, education, self-respect, and a belief in America. Unfortunately, that's not the kind of parents or world I grew up in. I believe in every word he says, but not all of us have the kind of parents or home environment that Colin was blessed with. If you're currently codependent or have been healed of codependency like me, you didn't get good parents (more than likely) or a good home environment. You may have gotten the very opposite: codependent parents, missing fathers, traumas, and abuse, to name a few. You may have been born into poverty, cotton fields, slavery quarters, or, like Christ, a manager. So, regardless of your upbringing or home environment, either good or bad, you stuck with it number one, but you are not a VICTIM. You can change your life like I did, but ONLY, I said only with professional help and GOD! You can turn your life around like I did with help. I promise you because I did, and so can YOU!

I just want desperately to help anyone like me (I know there are others out there) like me who had a terrible childhood and adult life as well. Without help, you will wander in and out of toxic and dysfunctional relationships, enduring more pain, hurt, abuse, and disappointments. Like Dorothy in The Wizard of Oz, you will be in La La Land looking for a Wizard to help you and you may not be able to find, just more dysfunctional people you stumble on during this trip to OZ. Not only will it affect you, but now you're passing it down to your kids, too.

In closing, I suggest you get some real professional help to get rid of those codependency demons and ask God (whatever higher power you believe in) to help you heal! I also read a quote from Eleanor Roosevelt that said, "You have to accept whatever comes, and the only important thing is that you meet it with courage, and with the best, you have to give since you get more joy out of giving, a joy to others you should put a good deal of thought into the happiness that you are able to give. God Bless You All, and Thank You for reading and sharing this book. I pray it has helped you in your quest for freedom from the clutches of codependency.

Acknowledgement

I am so blessed. Thank you, Lord for helping me after I was healed from codependency to have found some of my talents. This one is writing, which has helped me on so many levels to grow, vent, and revisit hurt and pains in my past I could not face before now. Thank you, Lord, for doing that for me. Thank you, Lord, for blessing and helping other women (young and seasoned, never old) of all nationalities get assistance in healing themselves, too. If I have been a source of information, teaching, and joy to anyone, I am proud that I've accomplished what I set out to do. Continue to pray for me and continue to get yourself help if you suffer like I did from codependency.

I read a quote by Jean Keir (l love to read) that said something so true in life, "As someone pointed out recently. If you can keep your head when all about you are losing theirs, it's just possible you haven't grasped the situation. Some people have such a talent for making the best of a bad situation that they go around creating them so they can make the best of them!"